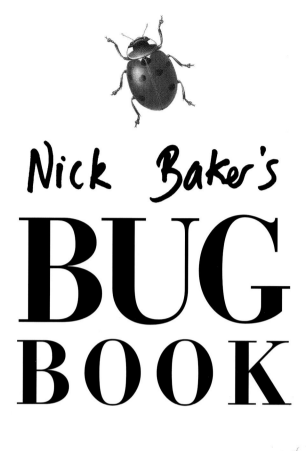

Nick Baker's
BUG
BOOK

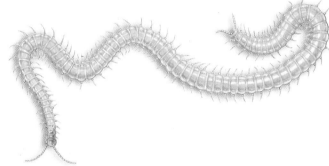

First published in 2002 by New Holland Publishers (UK) Ltd
London • Cape Town • Sydney • Auckland

2 4 6 8 10 9 7 5 3 1

Garfield House, 86-88 Edgware Road, London W2 2EA, United Kingdom
www.newhollandpublishers.com

80 McKenzie Street, Cape Town 8001, South Africa

Level 1/Unit 4, 14 Aquatic Drive, Frenchs Forest, NSW 2086, Australia

218 Lake Road, Northcote, Auckland, New Zealand

ISBN 1 85974 895 3 hardback

Publishing Manager: Jo Hemmings
Project Editor: Lorna Sharrock
Editorial Assistant: Daniela Filippin
Copy Editor: Sylvia Sullivan
Preliminary editorial liaison: Mike Unwin
Designer: Alan Marshall
Assistant Designer: Gulen Shevki
Index: Janet Dudley
Production: Joan Woodroffe

Reproduction by Modern Age Repro Co Ltd, Hong Kong
Printed and bound in Malaysia by Times Offset (M) Sdn Bhd

Nick Baker's
BUG
BOOK

Discover the world
of mini-beasts!

NEW HOLLAND

Contents

The Wildlife Trusts 7

Introduction 8

What Exactly is a Bug? 10

The Essential Bug-hunting Kit 12
A few rules • The eyeball • The kit • Making your bug restrainer • Making your pooter

Worms – The Hardest Working Inverts on (or under) the Earth 18
Celebrity status • What is a worm? • Body design • Hairy worms • Tunnel wizards • X-rated annelid • Making your wormery • The worm's turn • What eats worms? • Field guide

Slugs and Snails – Little Belly Feet 28
Slime appeal • Body design • Breathing pore • Making molluscs • Escargot on the menu • Experiment: To breathe or not to breathe? • Experiment: Slime surfing • Experiment: Watch 'em chomp! • Field guide

Arthropods, Starting with Woodlice 38
Suits of armour • Woodlice • Body design • I sentence you to 'death by vacuum cleaner'! • Experiment: Stinky pigs • Experiment: Give 'em a choice • Weird friends, cool enemies • Field guide

Centipedes and Millipedes – Loads of Legs 46
A wealth of walking gear • Frantic centipedes • Mooching millipedes • Lots of segments • Body design • Field guide

Arachnids – Things with Eight Legs! 50
Spiders • Body design • Know your way around a spider • The famous eight • Why are spiders hairy? • Spider vagabonds – wolf spiders • Experiment: Feel the vibe • The second half • Web spinning • Surfing the web • Making your 'tegenarium' • Experiment: Anyone for tennis? • Experiment: Finders keepers • Field guide

Introducing the Insects 66
Body design

Butterflies and Moths – Flights of Fancy 68
Butterfly or Moth? • A word on nets • Metamorphosis or magic? • Walking stomachs • Act Three • Lifecycle • Experiment: Digging in the dirt • Flamboyant finale • Wings – not just for flying! • Make a butterfly decoy • Experiment: All sweetness... • Making your sugaring for moths • Experiment: ... and light! • Making your moth trap • Orange tip butterflies • Keeping and culturing • Making your caterpillar box • Field guide

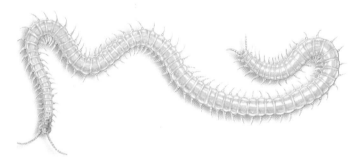

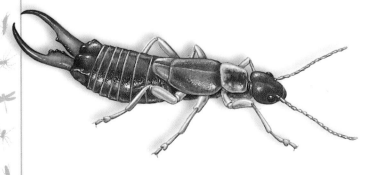

**Dragonflies and Damselflies –
'Here there be Dragons' 86**
The hardware • Telling them apart • The double
life of a dragonfly • The secret life of the
dragonfly • Behaviour to look out for •
Body design • Dragon hunting • Exuviae •
Experiment: Hatching your own

**Crickets and Grasshoppers – The Frenetic
Fiddlers 92**
It's simply not cricket • Body design • Grassroots
symphony • Perfect miniatures • Bush cricket
lifecycle • Cricket season • Shed light on a secret

**Wasps – Striped Hunters with a
Sweet Tooth 98**
High society • Inside the wasp factory • Strange
fruit • Wrapping it up • Going for galls •
Going it alone • The trackers

The Buzz about Bees 104
The sharp pointy end! • The good bit... • Body
design • Life styles of the socialites •
Experiment: Bee school • Early starters •
Temperature control • Bee cycle • Bee bank •
Making your bee box

Planet of the Ants 110
What is an ant? • Life cycles • What do
ants eat? • Making your formicarium •
Ant armoury • Recruitment and communication

Bugs – A Shed Load of Suckers! 118
Body design • What is a bug? • Bug lifecycle •
Greenfly on a stick! • Experiment: Bubble
bum • Water bugs • Buggles – the aeronauts

**The Beetles – Too Many Species, Too Little
Time 124**
Perfect cover • Demons in the dust • Little ladies •
Experiment: Rearing them • Falling for it •
Experiment: Making your pitfall trap • Beetles
about • Stars in the grass

True Flies and their Look-alikes 130
Body design • Mayflies, caddisflies and
stoneflies • Experiment: Catching water babies •
The tail of the scorpion fly • Lacewings

The Little 'uns 136
Body design • Making your tulgren funnel

Further Reading 138
Useful Addresses 140
Glossary 141
Index 142
Acknowledgements 144

The Wildlife Trusts

The Wildlife Trusts partnership is the UK's leading voluntary organisation working, since 1912, in all areas of nature conservation. We are fortunate to have the support of over 365,000 members, including some famous household names – such as Nick Baker.

The Wildlife Trusts protect wildlife for the future by managing more than 2,400 nature reserves, ranging from woodlands and peat bogs, to heathlands, coastal habitats and wild flower meadows; all good bug habitats!

We campaign tirelessly on behalf of wildlife, whatever their size and "love-ability". Whilst often associated with the more cuddly species such as the Otter, Red squirrel or Dormouse, we are active in our battle to protect invertebrates. Of the UK's 50,000 or so terrestrial and freshwater species, around three-fifths (30,000) are invertebrates.

Following the 1992 Rio Earth Summit the Government has given us lead responsibility for ten invertebrate species under the UK Biodiversity Action Plan process. They include the stunning Southern damselfly, Mire pill beetle, Narrow-headed ant and Black bog ant. One species, *Cryptocephalus exiguus*, is so rare it doesn't even have an English common name!

We run thousands of events and projects across the UK for adults and children. Our junior branch Wildlife Watch, which boasts Nick Baker as its vice president, regularly introduces youngsters and their families to the wonderful world of mini-beasts. Invertebrate species all have a part to play as pollinators of plants, decomposers of waste and as a food source for other creatures. They can also tell us a lot about the health of the environment.

We are working hard to attract more funding for invertebrate conservation, to protect habitats, to increase awareness of the value and importance of invertebrates and record species, and to persuade landowners to adopt invertebrate-friendly management regimes.

Many of these weird and wonderful creatures are under increasing threat – thank you for your interest in them and their plight. We hope you enjoy reading *Nick Baker's Bug Book* as much as we, at The Wildlife Trusts, have!

The Wildlife Trusts partnership is a registered charity (number 207238). For membership and other details, including Wildlife Watch, please complete and send the Direct Debit form, or phone us on 0870 0367711, or log on to www.wildlifetrusts.org

Introduction

If you find yourself irritating your relatives, prodding the cat or just plain bored out of your skull – then here's some therapy for you. What I'm going to shout about within these pages is all found within the boundaries of the average garden, park or patio. Everywhere around us there are myriad microcosms of mini-beast life; often completely overlooked by us all.

Get down and dirty your knees and that world of dots with legs and wings becomes tottering robots, oozing aliens, science fiction that is fact! These creatures fight their own little earth-moving battles while armed to the compound eyes with more weapons, poisons and nasty chemicals and tactics than you would have imagined could ever sit on a postage stamp. The world of the invertebrate is also smattered with fascinating mechanisms, gadgets, stunning colours, shapes and plenty of weirdos.

Out there dancing in the wind, mooching in the leaf litter, among your rockery and even in your pond or water butt is a world of tiny animals; small they may be, but their effects (and not just their deleterious ones) are noticed by us all.

These small denizens of the grassroots jungle run the planet, like 'em or not. Without them there wouldn't be

Above: *With the right equipment and a little bit of patience you can zoom in on the world of bugs.*

flowers or fruit, any of the fluffed and feathered animals that are more popular with the human masses and without their composting services we would be knee deep in dead leaves, dung and dead animals. Nice thought!

The 'Bug Effect'

A small word of warning that concerns the 'bug effect'. Show an insect, spider or any mini-beast for that matter to the uninitiated and you will find people are often sent legging it into another room, flailing arms and legs and generally making more noise than the size of the creature seems to justify. This reaction has been used by small children since time immemorial to frighten their family and friends. Sadly it is an easy trick and one that does nothing for the reputation of the harmless multi-legged creature sitting in the palm of the hand.

Above: *Hoverflies in a poppy. It is the scale of invertebrates that makes them fascinating; they fit so much into so little. Just peer into any flower and you can encounter an orgy of pollination, the occasional murder and a lot of sex!*

If you are a practical joker do not fall into the temptation of scaring the living daylights out of people. Instead try to understand that not all people you know are likely to be fond of invertebrates and are even less likely to understand your love of them. You can always attempt to talk people around to your own way of thinking – after all I managed to get my own mum, a serious arachnophobe, to hold one of my pet tarantulas. But be prepared for a long wait or complete failure – for some people it is simply too late!

If nothing else, this book will help you realise the place that many of the mini-beasts have in the whole scheme of things and that even if worms are not your 'cup of tea' you can sure bet that something that eats them is, be it badger or bird. It's the little things that make the world go around and even if this book makes you think twice about obliterating a beetle with your boot as it scampers across your path, then it has achieved something.

What Exactly is a Bug?

Bug, mini-beast, creepy-crawly are interchangeable friendly names used to describe any one of an enormous number of smallish life forms we find scuttling, oozing, creeping, flying and crawling through every ecosystem on the planet. Depending on where you come from and what your opinion is these names can refer to a huge range of different animals from true insects to centipedes, spiders and even slugs and snails!

These terms can refer to any small animal found on land or fresh water that is not warm-blooded and isn't a reptile or an amphibian! Between them, they look like a collection of extras from a science fiction movie. They range in size from the microscopic nematode worms to the massive (well relatively) 17 cm long, 100 g giant, the Goliath beetle! Some have one foot, others have six, eight, fourteen and even seven hundred and fifty legs! And some have bodies made of segments whereas others are encased in an armoured shell.

The one thing they do all have – or rather don't have – in common is a backbone. In fact, none of them have a single bone in their bodies and are called invertebrates by scientists, which translates to 'without a back bone'.

Broad-bodied chaser

Common azure damselfly

What is this book all about?

This is not supposed to be one of those books that lists, categorises and goes into great detail about what each animal is and who it's related to.

For a start, there are over 24,000 species of insect in the UK alone! To write about all of them and every other invertebrate you might stumble across I would have to be sitting in-doors in front of this laptop writing for many lifetimes without ever once stepping outside to swing a butterfly net or suck on a pooter! And where is the fun in that?

Whether they are making me mad by destroying my cabbages or making me gasp as an ugly nymph splits open and out crawls a dragonfly – invertebrates are out there to be enjoyed. That is, I hope, what this book is about – enjoying their lives.

Throughout these pages I will try and mention and feature as many of what I think are the sexy ones, the ones you should look out for and the ones you cannot fail to notice. There will be tips at least to recognising animals belonging to each rough group and telling them apart from other groups but that

**A centipede –
*Necrophloeophagus
longicornis***

is about as technical as I'm going to get. For the most part I will concentrate on little tricks, observations and backyard science that I have collected during my life as a 'bug man', all of which are aimed to help make a bit more sense of their sometimes complicated little lives.

As you dip in and out of the book or gaze at the contents list you will notice the book falls into three sections.

The first concerns animals that have no legs but still count as creepy-crawlies

Lesser stag beetle

or mini-beasts, such as worms, slugs and snails.

The next section contains animals that are arthropods (that is they have jointed legs but are not insects), such as woodlice, centipedes, millipedes, spiders and relatives.

And the final part is a huge section on insects, running through some of the commoner ones like butterflies, moths, dragonflies, damselflies, crickets, grasshoppers, wasps, bees, ants, bugs, beetles, flies and so on.

The vast variety of mini-beasts you could find in your garden

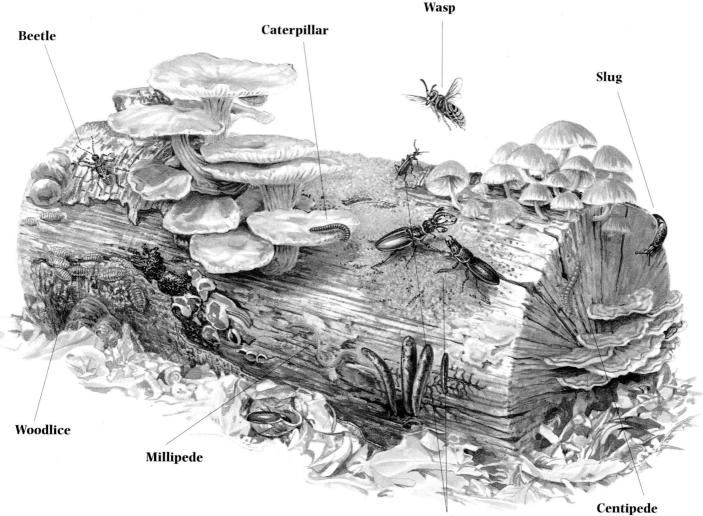

Wasp

Caterpillar

Beetle

Slug

Woodlice

Millipede

Beetles

Centipede

The Essential Bug-hunting Kit

One of the best things about invertebrates is that they are everywhere. If you are into 'bugs' you will never, ever be bored again, I guarantee it!

Above: Keep your eyes on the bug. It's all about how you look at the world around you. Here I am with all sorts of gadgets and tricks to enhance this ability.

Whether you find yourself in a car park or one of the best nature reserves this country has to offer, bugs will be there to be marvelled at and studied. The next best thing about bugs is that they are cheap. You really do not need any expensive equipment to get to know them. Always carry a notebook and pencil to make notes and sketches.

For the price of a cinema ticket you can have all you need to meet more weird and wonderful life forms up close than you could ever pack into a big budget science fiction film. I'm serious – there is no need to sensationalise here. Armed with little more than a magnifying lens, you can be stared back at by 36,000 eyes, observe virgin birth in your herbaceous border and experience a world of the most perfect and intricate details, colours and mechanics anywhere on Earth.

A few rules ...

Insects, Arachnids and their kin get a rough deal from us humans. We all know people who will douse them with toxic chemicals without so much as a second thought. Others will, without a flinch, put the boot in first and ask questions later. We also accidentally 'murder' millions every day – just check out the grill of a car on a summer's day.

Despite all this carnage, deliberate and otherwise, as a budding bug scientist you must ensure that you treat invertebrates with respect. Be gentle with them, let them go once you have finished observing their lives and disturb them as little as possible. Here are a few guidelines to keep you and your bugs happy.

1 Be calm, walk quietly and do not cause a hullabaloo. This is general good advice for any naturalist – you simply see more, and small animals do not always leg it for the nearest bush, hole or tree!

2 Always return stones and logs to their original position. How would you like it if a giant got you out of bed early, picked you up and then left your house on its side or in the next street!? Also if you are returning an animal to its hidden home put the stone, rock or log in place first and place your mini-beast next to it – it will find its own way back and it won't get accidentally squashed.

3 If you set a trap, particularly a pitfall trap (see page 127), make sure you check it at least once a day to save any bugs you find from dying.

4 If you hold on to a mini-beast for study, take care of its creature comforts – make sure there is a source of moisture, suitable food, shelter and something absorbent to soak up water droplets or condensation – the cause of the demise of many bugs is by drowning.

5 Never leave any captive mini-beast – even those that seem to like the heat – in direct sun. In fact it is good practice to avoid any extremes in temperature.

6 Invertebrates can live on very little oxygen and will survive in air-tight observation pots for a considerable time. However, if you are keeping them for any more than an hour, make sure there is plenty of ventilation. If you are keeping them for long-term study, remember it's better to look after a few well, than many badly!

7 Avoid directly holding or touching invertebrates with your hands – damage can be caused by clumsy fingers. Scales and hairs rub off and they will be sorely missed by the owner, and they may even die as a result.

8 Keep a record of what you've found by taking notes and making sketches of your mini-beast.

9 Always return any captive animals to exactly where you found them.

The eyeball ... the best, most valuable, essential, irreplaceable bug-hunting tool

Before we even get into the world of equipment and hunting techniques, the most important tool for the budding bug hunter is not his or her carbon-fibre butterfly net handle, nor the glossiest field guide with thumb index and Teflon pages, nor even a treble-coated, chromium-plated hand lens ... oh no. The single most useful tool that it is essential to learn to use right is staring right back at you when you look in the mirror. That's right – to be a good mini-beast scientist you need, above all else, to be able to use your eyes!

This may seem easy, but you will be surprised how many people can go for a walk in a meadow and see nothing, while the well-trained observer of all that sculks, scuttles and scurries can spend all day staring at a square metre of lawn and never be bored once! Never underestimate the power of your eyes.

Getting bugs in perspective

Just try lying in the long grass of a hay meadow on a sunny summer or spring day and looking through the grass blades. To start with you will see nothing but grass, but slowly you will feel a change in your focus. Instead of a few grass stems you will start to see a wild jungle of plants, a weird grass-roots world – ladybirds murdering greenflies, odd-looking bugs with strange mouthparts prodding and poking, giant stilt-walking spiders and harvestmen spanning gaps in the canopy while ants busily shuttle seeds and insects up and down from the dark forest floor to the top of the stems – the place is alive. Stand up and think about it, think of that little patch and then look out in front of you – there is an awful lot more grass out there and many more strange life forms to discover. You are now using your eyes correctly and are ready to embark on your exploration of the world both creepy and crawly!

Up close and personal
To be able to look an ant directly between the compound eyes, or appreciate how furry a spider is or even watch a woodlouse breathing – you need a magnifying hand lens. Of all the gear and gadgets you could own, this is the only one you cannot make and it is worth spending a little money on a good one. (Details of a few entomological suppliers can be found on page 140.)

There are many different kinds: high magnification (x20), low magnification (x5), big 'Sherlock Holmes' types, small pocket ones, metal or plastic, some with glass lenses, some with plastic and some with a choice of magnification!

All of them will be of some use. I prefer the small metal ones that fold up, especially those with two lenses, a x5 and a x10 are the most useful. The advantage of this sort is that they are lightweight – you can put them on a string around your neck – and because the lenses fold up within a protective case they are less likely to be scratched and damaged if you have a little accident as a result of over-zealous net swinging!

Magnifying hand lens

The kit ...

Pin 'em down!

As you begin studying mini-beasts you will soon realise one of the biggest frustrations with these animals is the way they move – for most, this means fast! Sometimes even if you have the creature captive in a pot, it will often be sprinting about so quickly it's hard to tell what colour it is, let alone how many legs it's got.

What you need is a bug restrainer. I know it sounds like a medieval torture device, but it is quite harmless and gentle if used correctly. It can help both you and the creature in question – you get to look at it close up and the animal gets released quicker because you are not going to hold it for hours in a jam jar.

See panel below.

You will need:
- *2 plastic drinking cups*
- *polystyrene tile*
- *marker pen*
- *scissors*
- *PVA glue*
- *cling-film*
- *elastic bands/tape*
- *hand lens*

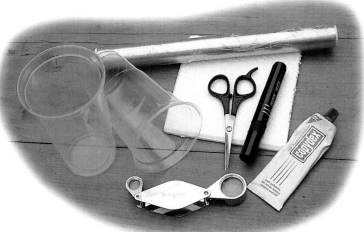

Making your bug restrainer

1 Take one of the cups and cut the middle out of the bottom leaving a rim. This is cup 'A'.

2 Stretch a piece of cling-film over the base and the hole in cup 'A' then secure it with either tape or elastic bands.

3 Take the other cup, this is cup 'B', and draw around its base onto the polystyrene tile, then using the scissors cut out this disc and using the PVA glue stick it to the underside of the base of cup B.

4 Once the glue is dry, your bug restrainer is complete and ready to use. Simply place your hyperactive bug into cup A and then slowly and gently push cup B into cup A until the bug is sandwiched between the cling-film and the polystyrene. You can now investigate your specimen. It may take a couple of attempts to get your specimen in the best position.

A few other useful tips

- Once the bug is restrained, work quickly. Do what you have to do and then release it as soon as possible – cling-film can suffocate small animals.
- Always make sure your bug is dry, otherwise it will stick and get in a right mess. You may also get condensation, which will spoil your view.
- Never try to restrain a bug that looks like it will be bigger than the base of the cups when stretched out.

A couple of points

Tweezers or forceps are useful things. They come in a range of different sizes for all sorts of jobs – but for the bug hunter they are best reserved for gently manipulating situations – turning over a stinging nettle leaf to look on the other side, to pick an empty spider skin out of a web, or to lift a tough animal such as a snail, beetle or caddisfly nymph.

For handling small or delicate animals tweezers are a bad idea, because it is hard to judge just how much force you are exerting on a creature. For simply touching, unfolding and gently poking use cocktail sticks or large sewing needles.

Nets please!

Nets are really just an extension of your body, allowing you to catch things, where using your hands and arms you wouldn't stand a chance! Having said that it is easy to jump straight in and start swinging your net around like an axe-wielding mad man. This is never a good idea. Watch and learn about your subjects first and use a net only if you really have to, for example to identify something that never seems to settle down, to reach up high, to collect creatures that live in thick grass or even under water.

Pots of pots

Bug hunting and pots go together like sharks and teeth. You will find yourself becoming quite the connoisseur of pots. Realising caterpillar-raising potential in ice-cream boxes, finding a perfect egg incubator in a sweet box and being able to find a display case for all your empty spider skins in chocolate truffle packaging will over time become one of your well honed skills as a bug enthusiast.

Start collecting them now – you will never have enough. Clear straight-sided boxes are always the best for observation, but anything will do. The addition of a few ventilation holes or a scrap of netting and an elastic band means you can extend the versatility of even the photographer's humble empty film cartridge (a favourite of mine!). You do not even have to know a photographer – just pop along and grovel at your local photo-developing shop.

Other sources of the best in entomological ware include: clear boxes used to transport a Chinese take away, in-flight food containers, disposable milkshake cups from the burger joint and margarine containers. Have fun, experiment, improvise and enjoy recycling for your hobby!

3

4

Different nets do different jobs

- A strong white net, with a heavy frame makes a good sweep net, for 'swooshing' through vegetation, like grass or bushes.
- A lightweight black mesh makes a good butterfly or flying insect catching net.
- A thick strong net with big holes for drainage is a good pond net.
- A net with a jam jar placed at the bottom is an adaptation for collecting tiny pond animals and plankton.
- You can, of course, buy all of these from specialist shops but, with a little effort, a sewing kit and a garden cane, you should be able to come up with something. Be prepared to improvise: a sieve or a tea strainer on a pole make as good pond nets as they do kitchen utensils!

One for the little suckers

The other trouble with creepy-crawlies is that a lot of them are on the minuscule side of tiny! This can create a number of problems. For a start they are tricky to pick up and look at. Even a well handled pair of tweezers can leave these tiddlers with damaged or missing limbs and wings, which is clearly not good, and you might even leave them mortally wounded.

The other problem is that, like buses, you often get lots of them at the same time (if you get around to using a beating tray (see page 71) you will see what I mean!) and then they are more than likely to be running in all directions. In situations like these you need what we call a pooter.

This is a serious bit of kit (used by professional scientists) with a very funny name. You can buy them from entomological suppliers, but at a cost. However, they can be easily made and will cost pennies not pounds. Once you have made one of these, you can use it again and again.

Making your pooter

1 Take the pot and in a well ventilated place using the lit candle heat the tip of the meat skewer. This is a little tricky and hazardous so get help if needs be. Then using the hot tip of the skewer burn two holes, slightly less than the diameter of your plastic tubing (the tubes must fit snugly into the holes).

2 Cut the plastic tubing into two pieces, one 20 cm long, the other 30 cm long. Insert each into one of the holes in the plastic lid (run them under a hot tap if you have difficulties, it makes the plastic softer). Push them in so that they hang about half way into the jar.

3 On the shorter tube, tie a piece of muslin over the end in the jam jar. Secure it with an elastic band.

4 Put the lid back on the jar. Wrap a small band of coloured insulating tape around the end of the short bit of tubing – this is to remind you which tube to suck on. If you suck on the other one by mistake you could end up with a mouth full of bugs.

5 Test your pooter by practising on small pieces of paper. Suck on the end of the short tube, while directing the end of the long tube over the paper. Working a bit like a vacuum cleaner, a short, sharp, gentle suck will transport the small thing into the jar, the muslin on the end of the tube stops it going in your mouth.

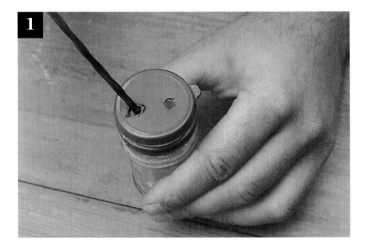

You will need:
- *Small jar with plastic lid (the kind you get herbs in is ideal)*
- *50 cm of clear plastic tubing – 5 mm in diameter (wine-making/DIY shops)*
- *coloured insulating tape*
- *elastic band*
- *a small piece of muslin or fine meshed fabric*
- *scissors*
- *candle*
- *matches*
- *meat skewer*
See panel below.

Spoon and paint brush

Many bugs have a really frustrating habit of folding up their legs and plummeting to the ground, on the slightest disturbance, in fact I'm sure some will do it if you just look at them! A cool trick here is the use of a table spoon. You can use this to catch the evading bug. If you combine this with a small camel-hair paint brush to sweep or flick delicate creatures off plants or the ground then you are bound to catch something.

For those still squeamish about picking up slugs and snails then two spoons can be used to pick these up in the same way you would spoon up sticky syrup.

A guide to good 'pootering'

- Only suck up small animals in your pooter. Anything fragile, with long legs or with a body nearly as wide as the tube will get stuck, be damaged or die.
- Try to keep the collection jar free from moisture. Do not blow into the tubes as this only fills it up with moisture from your breath.
- Wet and slimy animals such as slugs and snails are not good to 'poot' up as their mucus makes everything sticky.
- Try to keep the number of animals in the collecting jar to a minimum. Keep predators such as spiders away from other animals, as they could well eat your other specimens.
- Suck gently – soft, fragile animals can be injured if they are sucked up too violently – treat them gently and use short, sharp gentle sucks to get the pooter to work best.

Worms – The Hardest Working Inverts on (or under) the Earth

You have probably seen countless numbers of worms and not so much as blinked an eyelid at one, let alone ever been amazed by it. But despite their small size, slimy appearance and complete lack of any features that we can relate to, worms are very, very successful animals. However, do not just take my word for it, look at the fossil record for proof – worms have been making burrows and holes in planet Earth for some 120 million years!

Above: *Brandling worms. What you are looking at here is a bunch of very successful creatures! If you cannot appreciate the recycling, drainage and soil engineering work they do, simply look at them as dinner for many of the country's most exciting birds and mammals.*

Miles of burrows

Every acre of grassland can contain up to three million earthworms and each year between them they will turn over and mix up ten tons of soil! It has been estimated that every day this number of worms can make nine miles of burrows!

Celebrity status

These lean, largely unseen, tunnelling machines are vital to the health of your garden and other ecosystems on the planet. This important attribute of the earthworm has been realised, publicised and shouted about by many famous fans in the past.

Just some of the historical big celebrity names a worm could drop include Charles Darwin, who went so far as to say that worms were among the most important animals on the planet and wrote a book on them after spending 39 years studying worms (so I guess he should know!). Other worm-lovers include the Greek philosopher, Aristotle, who called worms the 'intestines of the soil' and even the Egyptian queen, Cleopatra, who thought worms were sacred (my kind of girl!).

The reason for this high-powered pro-celebrity following is that all these people realised that worms play an essential role in keeping the very soil we stand on in good condition. When the soil is good so is the plant life and everything that feeds on it.

Part of the reason worms are so influential lies in their numbers. There are an awful lot of them. As well as turning over or turning under the soil, worms break down plant material into a compost-like humus, make it easier for plants to have access to minerals, neutralise the acidity or alkalinity of the soil, allow air and water to pass freely through the earth, and provide food for many more obvious furry and feathery animals. You have definitely got a hard-working and astonishing invertebrate here!

So next time you see a worm struggling across a path, just remember that the animal you are looking at is not just a worm but a living, breathing, rotovating, composting, fertilising, soil shifting, drainage engineer!

What is a worm?

Look at a worm. It belongs to a group of animals known as *Annelids*, the segmented worms and, as their name suggests, all of these animals have a body divided into segments. As well as earthworms this group includes animals you might find at the seaside, such as ragworms and also the pond-loving leeches.

The segments on an earthworm can be seen very easily – dividing the body, so it looks a bit like a vacuum cleaner tube. This long stringy physique has lots of advantages.

As an animal a worm has the profile of a tube train! Being long, and flexible in all directions, it can squeeze between particles of soil or vegetation. It can also move forward by a series of muscular bulges. It appears slimy

Above: *Learn the worm. What am I doing? Well, I'm the proud owner of a 'wormery' that I've just made and soon I'll have a private window into their secret underworld.*

because it secretes a thick mucous from glands on its surface. In the same way as oil allows a piston to slide easily up and down in its case, this slimy mucous allows the worm to move through its burrows. At the same time it acts like cement, binding together loose soil particles and it slows down the loss of water through the skin when conditions are a bit on the dry side.

Body design

Saddle or clitellum? – This is only found in fully grown up worms. It plays an important part in worm reproduction (see pages 21–2).

Mouth – The only recognisable feature on a worm's 'head', and you have to look very closely to see it, the mouth lies just under the tip of its snout.

Head or tail? – Because worms do not have a 'face' as such, they have no eyes, ears and no obvious nose. The easiest way to tell a worm's head from its tail is to watch which way it crawls. If your worm is inactive then the thin round end is the head and the flattened paddle-shaped end is the tail.

Tail

Head

Sensitive souls – You can't see them but a worm has lots of tiny 'taste buds' all over its body but particularly on its 'head end', something like 700 per square millimetre. That is why worms are able to find food, despite not having any eyes. They are also very sensitive to touch and have many nerve endings just under their skin. The bristles or setae double up as vibration sensors. Worms also have light-sensitive cells on their bodies.

Hairy worms!

Have you ever seen a blackbird, thrush or robin struggling to pull a worm from its burrow in the lawn? How can the worm put up such a fight? Well, next time you find an earthworm that is active, try holding it in your clenched fist – you will feel just how strong a worm is as it tries to force its way between your fingers. It uses all those muscles to push and pull its body through the soil. But that isn't the whole story.

Earthworms are grouped together with some 3,000 or so different kinds of worms known as *Oligochaetes* – that sounds complicated but translated it means 'few bristles'. If you place a worm on a piece of paper, you

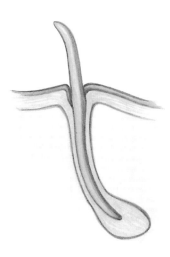

Right: *This is one of the many bristles or setae that protrude from the side of the worm's body. They feel rough if you draw the worm backwards through your fingers.*

may be surprised at the noise it makes as it moves; not a squishy slurpy noise but a dry scratchy one and if you gently pull a worm backwards between your fingers you will feel a roughness on the worm's skin.

Both of these seemingly weird worm phenomena are caused by lots of tiny bristles (four per segment) called setae. The worm uses these to grip the walls of its tunnel to help it move through the soil and it is these same little bristles that give worms a fighting chance in that deadly tug-o-war with garden birds!

Above: *Mistle thrush. Earthworms have had 120 million years of bigger creatures trying to pull them out of their burrows, being hunted and eaten. You simply do not get this far without a few survival tricks up your sleeve.*

Tunnel wizards

Place a worm on the soil and within minutes it has forced its way below, into its dark damp world. How on earth does it dig?

Despite not having any arms and legs, worms progress through the soil in a number of ways. Their body design, a long, segmented tube, is very flexible and

Charming worms

This has nothing to do with their charisma as sadly worms do not have an awful lot of this. They tend to exist and then get eaten – sort of disposable animals. It seems that nearly any animal with a penchant for invertebrates eats worms. Worm-eating animals have lots of different ways of catching these subterranean beasts, but one of the most ingenious is one you can replicate yourself.

'Puddling' is behaviour that certain smart birds, particularly gulls, engage in. Watch them on damp short grass, on overcast days – playing fields are a good place to keep an eye open for this behaviour. The birds appear to be doing an on-the-spot jig, stepping up and down on the same spot repeatedly. What they are actually up to is convincing the worms to come to the surface. Why the worms oblige is a bit of

a mystery, but the gull stamping produces vibrations to which the worms are very sensitive. To the worm this 'drumming' could sound a bit like rain – and worms tend to surface in the rain perhaps because conditions above the surface suddenly become more favourable for them or simply to escape water-logged burrows. Whatever the reason, come to the surface they do and dinner they become. Bizarrely, humans also do this – not for food but for a competition known as 'worm charming'! This involves stamping, patting, prodding and even watering the soil to get as many worms to surface in your square metre as possible. It works too, try it on your lawn or in the park – you may have to wait a while and people may ask questions but eventually you should be rewarded by a worm or two poking its head out of the grass!

stretchy. It is also very muscley. In fact your average *Lumbricus terrestris* (Common earthworm), with its 250-odd segments, probably has more muscles than Arnold Shwarzenegger! It has lots of ring-shaped ones that run around the body and long ones that run the length of its body. It can control these muscles in a very precise way. The body is also full of water (water makes up 70-95% of your average worm!). You can think of each segment as a tough balloon full of water. The great thing about water is that it cannot be squashed; try filling a balloon and squeezing it – when you push in one place the balloon expands and squishes out another way – it is impossible to make the volume of the water-filled balloon actually smaller. Combine the water and the muscles and you have a very impressive tunnelling machine indeed.

Using its muscles, the worm can make itself long and thin, squeeze into tight gaps between soil particles, and then use its muscles and that 'water balloon' effect to squash its segments up, causing its body to push apart the soil. By repeating this action, and using the setae or bristles to grip the soil, the worm can push and pull its way underground, and it smoothes its path by producing mucous.

X-rated annelid

How can you tell whether your earthworm is a he or a she? Well, that is very easy indeed. All earthworms are both! They are what is termed hermaphrodite, having

Above: *The sensual worm. Not shy, earthworms will do it on your lawn in full view of all that tread quietly and are armed with a red torch (see* Worms in the dark *below).*

both male and female reproductive parts. Despite this, one worm does need another.

The theory behind all this is that being small creatures worms probably rarely bump into each other so having both male and female bits means that if one worm does encounter another, both animals benefit twice, they both get sperm and they both fertilise their eggs, effectively doubling their money!

Have a look at your worms – do they have what looks like a big, fat often pale segment approximately two thirds of the way down the body? If so they are grown up worms. Only mature worms have a 'saddle' like this, also called a clitellum. It's used as part of the worms' slimy embrace, when they meet and mate, producing a blanket of thick mucous. If you go out on warm, wet summer nights armed with a red cellophane-covered torch, search the lawn for worms lying next to each other, (it will usually be the big Common earthworm *Lumbricus terrestris*, as many other species

Worms in the dark

Like many nocturnal animals, worms cannot see red light, so cover torches with red cellophane if you want to watch them after dark.

mate underground). Tread carefully as you go about your business as they are really, really sensitive to vibrations caused by heavy footfalls. Put yourself in their holes – as far as they are concerned you could be a badger about to slurp them up!

If you find a pair of worms mating, you will notice one is facing one way, while the other faces the opposite direction. They are engaged in the worm equivalent of a hug. They grip each other with the long setae on the belly and to help even more, the clitellum produces a thick sticky sheet of mucous which looks and functions a bit like sticky tape, keeping them close.

Over the next two or three hours the worms transfer sperm and go their separate ways. During the following few days each worm will produce more mucous-like substances from their saddles, and in the same way as you peel a jumper off over your head the worm does this with this band of mucous and as it passes the male and female bits – sperm and eggs are placed in it. As it rolls over the worm's head, the ends seal to form what for all the world looks like a small lemon – this is the worm's egg cocoon which now waits to hatch. From up to 20 eggs only a few baby worms will successfully hatch.

Making your wormery

Most of what worms get up to happens far from curious eyes, below the surface of the soil. But you can make a study of worm behaviour with a simple but clever device called a 'wormery', an essential bit of kit for the Oligochaetologist (someone who studies worms).

You will need:
• *piece of 2 cm x 2 cm wood 116 cm long*
• *14 small wood screws*
• *2 pieces of clear Perspex (30 cm x 30 cm)*
• *30 cm strip of wood, 4 cm wide*
• *elastic bands*
• *a selection of different coloured soils, (garden soil, sand, potting compost)*
• *2 pieces of black card/paper 30 cm x 30 cm*
• *screwdriver*
• *drill*
• *scissors*
• *water*
• *5–6 worms*
See panel below.

Making your wormery

1 Cut the wood to lengths: 1 x 30 cm, 2 x 28 cm, 2 x 15 cm and place the pieces together.
2 Then using a drill, drill two holes a few cms from the corners on each edge and repeat on the other side. Also drill two holes in through one of the 28 cm piece of wood (these will eventually act as drainage holes) and a hole in each of the two remaining 15 cm pieces, which will eventually become the feet of the wormery.
3 Using the 14 screws, screw the whole contraption together as in the illustration. The wood should be sandwiched between the two pieces of Perspex, flush at the edges, the feet should be screwed on last.
4 Add the soils, one at a time in alternating layers, add a few leaves at the top and water lightly.
5 Add 5-6 worms and then place the 30 cm strip (4 cm wide) of wood on top, using the elastic bands to hold it in place. This acts as a lid and stops the worms escaping. Then place the two pieces of paper or card over the sides of the wormery and keep in a cool place. Remove the paper/card blinds when you want to observe the worms within.
6 Check daily to make sure the soil is damp, but never soggy and wet, adding water if necessary.

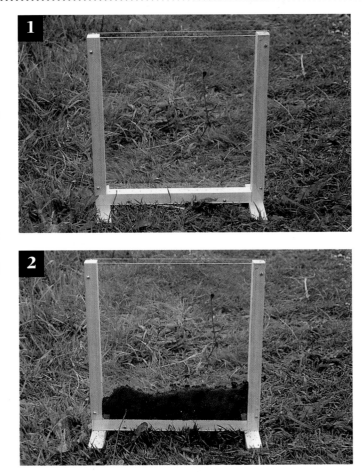

Right: *This is the most satisfying bit of making your wormery, adding the worms themselves. Do not forget to put a bit of cling film or wood over the top, otherwise your worms will do a runner!*

3

4

5

Worm cigars

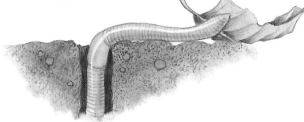

1 Gingerly and usually under the cover of darkness, the worm quests for its prize, keeping its tail anchored in its burrow for a quick retreat.

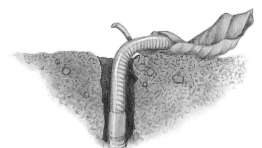

2 Having located a freshly fallen leaf, the worm grasps the stem in its minute mouth and drags the leaf back toward the burrow.

3 Pulling the leaf into its front door is a bit of a struggle, but the brute force of the strong little worm, results in the leaf folding and rolling into a cigar shape.

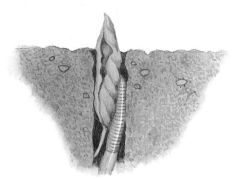

4 The leaf is often left to soften and decompose a little before the worm begins tucking it in the safety of its burrow. The nutrients in the leaf are returned to the soil.

Above: *On autumn days, as the leaves are falling, look at the surface of a lawn. The chances are you will find brown leaves, rolled neatly and stuffed in the ground. These 'cigars' are hand-rolled by earthworms.*

The worm's turn – what worms eat

Soil can be split into two main ingredients. The first is the hard stuff, which is made up of what was at one time rock. (Rocks are worn down by weather and water over time by a process known as erosion, to form lots of tiny microscopic particles.) The second ingredient is the part of the soil that is made from plants and animals that have rotted down. This is the magic stuff called humus, and it is humus that holds water, influences the texture of the soil and provides a lot of the nutrients that enable plants to grow.

This is where our earthworms step into the equation. Worms swallow soil as they go – they feed on the humus, removing what they need and what comes out the other end is broken down even further. Worms speed up the process of rotting or decomposition.

Have a close look at the surface of your lawn and you may notice what looks like hand-rolled cigars stuffed into tiny holes in the lawn! What on earth has been going on here?

Well, look for clues and you may see that surrounding some of these 'cigars' are worm casts.

To find out what has been going on here you need to be a nocturnal nature detective. Armed with a torch covered with red cellophane (remember worms are blind to red light) go out on a warm, wet autumn night and scour the lawn for worm action. You may find worms mating (see page 21) or if you are really lucky you may catch a worm reaching out of its burrow with its front end, grabbing a leaf in its mouth and pulling it

Above: *Probably the most aesthetically-pleasing poo in the world. The worm cast is in fact not at all unpleasant. It is just partially digested soil full of goodness for your lawns and plants.*

by its stem into the burrow. Here the leaf will naturally fold and roll to fit the hole. The worm covers it with digestive spittle and waits until it has softened before starting to eat it. By doing this, the worm is fertilising your soil and speeding up the composting process of the leaf. This is why raking up leaves and tidying the lawn in autumn is bad for worms and bad for gardens! If you left the leaves long enough, most would end up buried in the lawn – think of all the raking and sweeping that would save!

Cast away

What exactly are those strange wiggly things that seem to spring up all over lawns? Well, there is no polite way of saying it, this is actually worm poo! To be precise it is the excrement of one of two species, *Allolobophora longa* and *A. nocturna*, which between them are almost entirely responsible for all the worm casts that appear on the surface. Other species produce them, but they normally remain in the entrance of the burrow.

Do not worry about all this worm dung, it is not very unpleasant. Take some and rub it between your fingers and you will notice it is made of lots of tiny particles of soil. In fact that is pretty much what it is. The worms swallow soil and digest some of the organic stuff, humus, that is rotten plant and animal material. The great thing about worms is that they are so inefficient at digesting that if you were to analyse the contents

of a worm cast you would find it contains 65–70% humus. This is good news because as it passes through the worm's body it is broken down into smaller pieces and a lot of the goodness it contains is now available for plants to feed on – it is fertiliser!

Badger snacks

The menu of some badgers can contain 70% or more worms!

False pride?

There are a few people who are so proud of their manicured lawn that they hate worms messing it up with their casts, so they poison the soil and kill all the worms. This is not very wise; not only is it bad news for the worms but in killing them all the gardener is committed to a life of hard work. To stop the grass dying the gardener now has to do the same work the earthworms were doing before. He has to spend a lot of time spiking the lawn to allow water to drain away and air to get to the grass roots. He also has to spend time and money adding fertiliser to the grass, to

Below: *In one end and out the other, as the worm tunnels it swallows the soil, digesting and absorbing what it needs. The rest is expelled at the surface as a squiggly worm cast.*

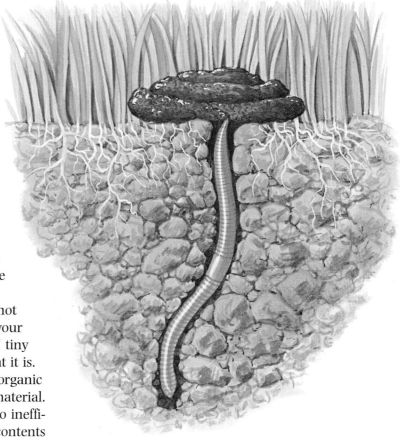

Long lived

Assuming that they stay out of the way of worm gobblers, Common earthworms can live for around ten years!

What eats worms?

If after all this you are still not a big fan of worms then at least you should have realised how the planet would be a much duller place without them. If you start thinking about worms as food, they are ideal – small, no tough chewy bits, easy to digest, high in protein and, if you know where to look, there are plenty of them.

Not surprisingly, many animals have sussed this out. Watch birds on sports fields – gulls, rooks, starlings, blackbirds, thrushes and robins are just a few of the common birds that eat a lot of earthworms.

Others with a penchant for these wigglers include birds like Curlews, even big birds of prey such as Buzzards enjoy them. Then there are the mammals such as Hedgehogs, shrews, Moles and Badgers, which eat so many worms that they deserve the title of 'wormivore'. There are slugs and some leeches that will eat worms and millions of them are hung on fishing hooks every year to tempt a trout or two.

If you are jealous of these animals and their nutritious fodder, there's no need. Historically, humans ate worms and still today there are people, other than the occasional experimental baby, who enjoy sucking on an *Annelid*! Below is a real recipe for those wanting to complete their understanding and appreciation of worms.

replace the nutrients that are washed away by the rain. Before, the earthworms would have naturally compensated for this by bringing these same nutrients to the surface in their worm casts. So leave those earthworms alone!

Field guide to common worms

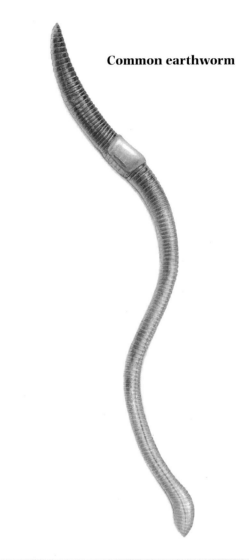

Common earthworm

Earthworm meatloaf

1.5lb / 750 g ground beef
1 cup boiled earthworms, finely chopped
1 packet dry onion soup mix
1 cup evaporated milk
1 bell pepper chopped
1 slice of fresh bread torn into bits

Mix all the ingredients together and place in a loaf tin. Bake for an hour at 200°C/400°F. I'm serious – it's good! For more real recipes see *The Worm Book* by Loren Nancarrow and Janet Hogan Taylor.

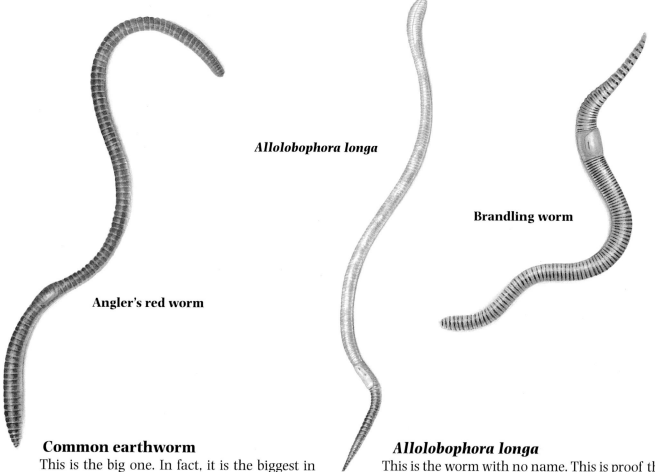

Allolobophora longa

Brandling worm

Angler's red worm

Common earthworm

This is the big one. In fact, it is the biggest in this country, growing to a length of 30 cm fully stretched out! This is my favourite. It has a healthy-looking pinkish glow to its body and a dark point to the head end and you can often see its blood vessels pulsating along its back! It is a powerful worm and I've heard it said that this champion digger is capable of moving stones so big that the human equivalent would be for us to shift a 2.5 ton weight!

These worms live in deep burrows and can dig down over a metre. They do not produce worm casts on the surface so unless you dig them up, you probably will not know they are there. However, this is the worm that you are most likely to encounter on the surface of the lawn on a warm, humid night. Because of this they have got another name, which is used a lot in America, of 'night crawler'.

Angler's red worm

Another lover of the compost heap and rich soil, this worm looks a bit like the common earthworm but it is smaller and redder with an oily iridescence to its skin surface. Also called a 'red wiggler' because on exposure to light it tends to throw its body into a fit of twisting and turning – a habit that makes them popular with fishermen! 2.5–14 cm in length.

Allolobophora longa

This is the worm with no name. This is proof that there is no justice in the world, because this worm is very common indeed and is famous for leaving those squiggly little sculptures on the surface of the lawn, the worm cast. It grows to 10–12 cm in length.

Brandling worm

Commonly called the tiger worm, this is a smallish worm, about 10 cm in length. This beast has a very distinctive stripy body alternating between the deep red of the segments and pale flesh between. Brandling worms are not fussy about where they live. They can tolerate big changes in temperature, acidity and wetness – as far as worms go these are tough nuts! Leave a pile of grass clippings to rot in your garden, turn it over a few months later and you will probably find these beasts. Or look in your compost heap.

The sickly worm?

Dendrobaena subrubicunda
Lift up a log or stone in woodland where there are rotting leaves and the chances are you will find this anaemic-looking chap. This worm doesn't look very well – it is short, stubby, pale and yellow in places.

Slugs and Snails – Little Belly Feet

Slugs and snails belong to a huge group of animals known as molluscs, which includes the clams, mussels, chitons, octopus and squid. Within this they belong to a class known as the Gastropods, which is a cool name that means 'belly foot'. This describes them very well as they all get around on a single, large, muscular foot, which sits underneath their whole body.

Slime appeal

Slugs and snails are not a very popular group of creepy-crawlies at the best of times. This is partly because they are badly misunderstood by most of us and we wrongly accuse all of them of liking our lettuce and strawberries and having a penchant for our pansies. They also have the unfortunate quality of being slimy. This really does do nothing for their appeal to us or to the average gardener.

Above: *Face to face with a snail. There's definitely something great about going around with your home on your back – a bit like going backpacking on holiday!*

Glands on the skin
The slime slows down the rate at which water is lost from the surface of their skin. Because slugs do not have a shell they are more vulnerable to desiccation, so they have much thicker slime. Having said that, some tough slugs and snails can lose around 50% of the water in their bodies and still survive.

Multi-purpose mantle
The mantle serves many purposes: it secretes the shell in snails and forms a curtain that the snail hides behind when it retreats into its own shell. It is also responsible for the screen of bubbles that are blown at any intruder or over-curious conchologist (someone who studies slugs and snails).

But get to know them and this group of some 100 or so different species in the British Isles (80 types of snail and around 20 slugs) are a fascinating bunch. Very few species actually cause damage to our plants and gardens and some are even quite pretty. They are all, however, quite slimy and this is for a good reason as I will explain later on.

Slugs and snails are much the same, the only real difference being that snails have a hard shell that they can withdraw into while slugs do not. However, there are slugs with tiny shells on their backs and most species have a little one inside their bodies and there are a few snails that do not fit inside their own shells too!

Shells – tough wrapper, survival suit
The purpose of the shell in snails is to protect them from predators and make them a difficult mouthful to swallow. It also acts as a kind of survival capsule. Slugs and snails lose a lot of water every day through their skin and the production of slime uses up a fair bit of water too, so they need to conserve it. Snails use their shell to

Body design of slugs and snails

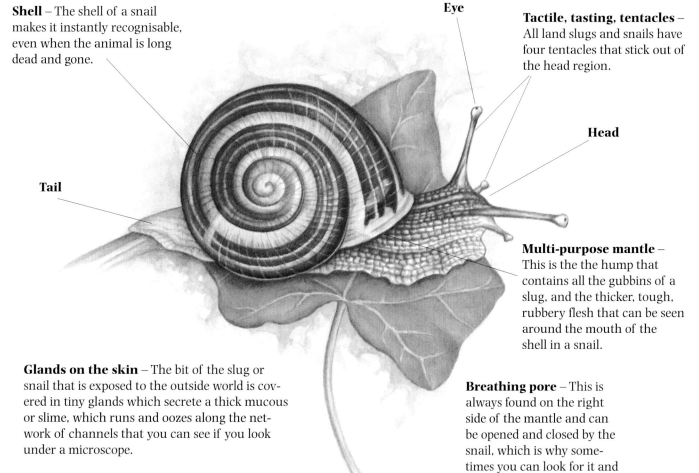

Shell – The shell of a snail makes it instantly recognisable, even when the animal is long dead and gone.

Eye

Tactile, tasting, tentacles – All land slugs and snails have four tentacles that stick out of the head region.

Head

Tail

Multi-purpose mantle – This is the the hump that contains all the gubbins of a slug, and the thicker, tough, rubbery flesh that can be seen around the mouth of the shell in a snail.

Glands on the skin – The bit of the slug or snail that is exposed to the outside world is covered in tiny glands which secrete a thick mucous or slime, which runs and oozes along the network of channels that you can see if you look under a microscope.

Breathing pore – This is always found on the right side of the mantle and can be opened and closed by the snail, which is why sometimes you can look for it and not find anything!

help them do this. Obviously slugs do not have this advantage and that is the main reason why you can find snails in drier habitats than slugs (before you start feeling sorry for slugs because they haven't got a shell, they can fit and squish into smaller tighter spaces than snails and they can move faster!). When conditions get really bad – very cold in winter or extremely dry in the heat of summer – snails can retreat into their shells and seal off the entrance with a thick mucous, which dries to form a waterproof seal that technical people call an epiphragm. You can often see this if you peel a snail off a dry wall in summer.

Wrinkles and rings
When trees grow they leave a pattern of growth rings inside their wood. These rings are formed when the tree has good times for growth and then bad times – usually summer and winter seasons. The same thing can be seen in snails. If you look at a snail's shell closely enough you will notice little ridges and sometimes a slightly different colour to sections of the shell.

Snails grow by adding new material to the mouth of the shell. This can be seen in early spring as they start growing, the lip of the shell is soft and almost papery. This can be explained by the way the shell is created. The shell is formed with two layers of building material: first, a horny outer layer that acts like a water proof varnish and, secondly, a tough chalky layer underneath. It's that first layer that appears papery and thin. In a similar way to trees, snails have good times, where food is plentiful and they grow well, followed by hard times like winter, or a really dry spell when the snail hardly grows at all. Boundaries between these periods are what causes the ridges and wrinkles in the shell.

Breathing pore

This hole leads to a chamber called the mantle cavity, which is used a little bit like a lazy lung. Air wafts in and all the oxygen the snail wants is picked up by a network of blood vessels in the skin. Some pond snails use this technique too. If you keep a few Great pond snails in a jam jar next to your bed at night you can actually hear them breathing, making a kind of popping noise as they come to the surface and open their breathing pore. Some other water snails have gills and fill their mantle cavity with water, from which they extract oxygen. Others have a combination of both.

All slugs and snails can also breathe through their skin (see Breathing experiment page 33).

Tactile, tasting, tentacles
Look closely and you will see that they each have a dark eye-spot right at the very tip – this is the eye, but it cannot see very much. It would be a bit like sticking greaseproof paper over your own eyes. You could see the difference between light and dark but that's about all!

However, snails are very sensitive to light and they use it to guide their way out of their daytime retreats, following the low light of the night out into the garden to feed. Tentacles are also used to feel their way around, they use them as you would use your hands if you were blindfolded. You can steer a slug or

Above: These two entwined slugs are in fact in their mating embrace, exchanging sperm. Definitely something to try and see by torchlight.

snail by gently touching the tentacles one side at a time. Each of the four tentacles is also covered in taste buds that allow the slugs or snails to taste and smell food. The lower ones are sensitive to food up to 20 cm away, while the two larger top tentacles work over longer distances of 50 cm or more. That's how slugs and snails sniff out your strawberries so effectively! Because they are so important to the mollusc, the tentacles can be protected by drawing them inside out and sucking them back into the body, in the same way a glove finger can be turned inside out. If you do not understand what I'm trying to say, watch them yourself. Gently tap a tentacle with your finger and watch as it rolls in on itself. When the coast is clear the mollusc squeezes blood back into them and they roll out again. If they do get damaged it still is not the end of the world as new ones grow to replace them!

Making molluscs

Like the worms in the previous chapter, there is no such thing as a he or she snail or slug! Each animal is both! Why? Well, it's helpful for such famously slow-moving animals. If they do bump into each other, they need to make the most of the moment and because both animals can mate and crawl away having been fertilised both parties are happy and can relax and get on with laying their eggs!

The act itself can be witnessed usually on a perfect slug and snail night, the conditions for love are damp, dark and warm. Take a torch – you never know what you might see. Snail and slug love can be as simple as a

Spectacularly sexy slug!

The Great grey slug has some of the most spectacular sex in the animal world and if you are ever fortunate enough to witness it you will feel like giving them a round of applause when they have finished. It goes a bit like this.

First the slugs meet, they run each other around and work up a bit of a lather, producing loads of mucous, then one slug initiates the act of 'going upstairs'. They climb up a vertical surface, still chasing each other. When they find a mutually acceptable spot for their affair they start tickling

each other with their tentacles. As they get more and more involved with each other they continue to ooze slime and further entwine until they make the ultimate lovers' leap!

This is more of a lovers' abseil really as they slowly lower themselves on a rope of slime, which can be as much as a metre long. It is at the end of this slime rope that their relationship is finally consummated.

kind of mollusc kiss chase, with one animal picking up the trail of the one it fancies and following it until the potential mate is found. Then after a quick (well quick for a mollusc!) embrace both animals are on their way having exchanged sperm via the genital pore on the side of their bodies.

Mollusc mating reaches another level of complexity with certain snails whose courtship is surprisingly passionate. When a Garden snail encounters a mate they meet each other head on, rear up and with their mouths pressed together they 'kiss' for a while. Then to get each other in the mood they fire 'love darts' at each other. I'm not kidding! After stabbing each other with these sharp shards of shell-like material, they mate. Nobody is really sure what these darts do; they could stimulate the other snail into producing sperm or they could inhibit the other snail from mating with another. I bet you never realised the amount of lust and passion that goes on in your herbaceous border, behind the flowerpots!

Egg fest

When you spend time poking around in the soil and exploring beneath bark and stones, sooner or later you will stumble upon what look like little clusters of miniature ping pong balls. These are the eggs of slugs and snails. They are laid in damp crevices where they are not going to dry out. Depending on the temperature, they will hatch within a few weeks. They are quite fun to collect and watch hatch. You will see the little molluscs inside the egg just before they break free.

The size of the clutch laid varies a lot, but anywhere between 10 and 100 eggs is common.

The eggs of pond snails are very different, they are usually found on pond weed or on the undersides of lily pads and stone surfaces. They differ from those of land snails in having a protective jelly coating.

Escargot on the menu

It's tough convincing some people that slugs and snails have their place in the world. A lot of people will, without thought, throw down slug pellets and slowly turn the subject of this chapter into a slimy lifeless blob.

Not nice for the slugs and snails, it may cure the problem of the nightly nibblers of our prized seedlings but for every one we maliciously murder in this way, I wouldn't mind betting there are several other animals going hungry that we would rather like to see in our gardens. Not every animal hates slugs: some, as we are about to find out, positively love them. But before we get off the subject of killing and poisoning slugs, remember that any that are slowly dying can be consumed by

Above: Helix aspersa *eggs. The eggs of the common Garden snail have the same translucence as light bulbs. I often stumble upon little clusters of between 10 and 100 snail eggs whilst digging the flowerbed or lifting stones and logs.*

other animals. By using chemicals and poisons on any pest, you could be poisoning animals you would love to have in your garden.

One of the top mollusc mashers leaves vital clues at the scene of the crime. Shards and splinters of snail shells scattered around prominent rocks, stones, paths and patios is the work of the Song thrush. This bird uses these 'anvils' to dash the snail's shell to pieces and get to the succulent morsel inside. Both Mistle thrush and Blackbirds also put away large numbers of slugs and snails. They just haven't invented such an effective way to get the wrappers off.

Look under corrugated tin sheets, often the home of Field and Bank voles. Here you will find neatly piled clusters of snail shells, stacked like broken crockery. Shrews and hedgehogs join the band of apparently harmless looking little fluffies that will snack on snails.

I once had a pet toad that was very fond of eating little white garden slugs. In the garden, toads provide a great slug removal service along with that legless lizard, the Slow worm.

Garlic snail

The Garlic snail, as its name suggests, tries to put off its attacker by smelling strongly of garlic!

or crunching through a snail shell like a pair of bolt cutters. Even worse than this is an animal that has an enviable, even a glowing, reputation. Glow worm larvae go about preparing their dinner in a particularly gruesome way. These unusual beetles prey almost entirely on slugs and snails. By repeatedly stabbing their victim with venom-laden mouthparts, they slowly paralyse the unfortunate mollusc and when it is not able to run away or even twitch, the young Glow worm larvae proceeds to eat the animal alive. This is enough to make even the most ardent slug and snail hater to start feeling sorry for them.

Above: *One very high profile ambassador for molluscs – the Hedgehog loves 'em even if you don't.*

Ghastly slug guzzlers!

All of the above slug guzzlers will eat the animals whole, but if you are one of these molluscs the last thing you really want to bump into in a dark alley way is a beetle. Ground beetles are equipped with a pair of large vicious-looking mandibles that are capable of slicing open a slug

Below: *Smash and grab. No prizes for table manners for the Song thrush. It beats the shell against a favourite rock or 'anvil' until it shatters. These sacrificial altars can be found surrounded with splintered shards of shell.*

In their defence...

After reading about the various grisly ways a slug or snail can leave this world you can mop up your tears – it's not all one way – slugs and snails can defend themselves very well. For a start, the obvious defence for a snail is to chicken out of a situation completely and withdraw its soft parts into its protective shell. Admittedly this is only a defence against animals that cannot open the shells, but if you pick up a snail and poke it, eventually it will belch forth an impressive quantity of bubbles. This sticky green froth gets everywhere and will certainly put off many predators, especially the vain ones that do not want to mess up their feathers and fur.

Slugs, despite appearing quite vulnerable without a shell, are not as defenceless as you might at first think. A slug that one moment is sliding along minding its own business, can hunch up into a ball shape in seconds. By doing this its tentacles are withdrawn and by pulling itself together in the face of fear it exposes a large hump of its mantle, which is covered in a thicker leathery skin.

This posture also has the effect of making the slug harder to pick up or bite into, especially when it starts to produce a

thicker slime in its defence. Try picking one up and you will find the goo is like glue.

I once performed an experiment with Great black slugs in my garden and put some out under the bird table. A Blackbird showed interest, but after picking one up once it soon lost interest and spent the next five minutes trying to wipe the mucous off its beak.

This same species of slug, when things get too much for it, also goes in for a bit of rocking. Quite how or why this is scary I'm not sure but it certainly looks fairly funny if you get a chance to see it happening.

Experiment: To breathe or not to breathe?

All slugs and snails can breathe to an extent through their skin as well as through their breathing pore. To prove this a simple experiment can be conducted with Great pond snails.

You will need:
• *2 identical jam jars*
• *water*
• *stopwatch or watch*
• *a kettle*
• *2 Great pond snails*

Above: *The Great pond snail, a common aquatic freshwater snail. They cannot breathe under water, a design fault perhaps for a water snail, but they seem to manage just fine returning to the surface to get a lung full of air.*

First take the two jam jars. Fill jam jar 'A' with normal water from the tap, then for the water in jam jar 'B' you need to remove most of the dissolved oxygen. You can do this by boiling water and allowing it to cool to the same temperature as the other (this is quite critical otherwise you will end up boiling your charges alive!).

Place a snail of about the same size in both jars. Then, using a stop watch, count the number of times and how long each snail spends at the surface with its breathing pore open. You should find that the snail in oxygen-poor water, jam jar B, needs to breathe at the surface more often than the snail in jam jar A.

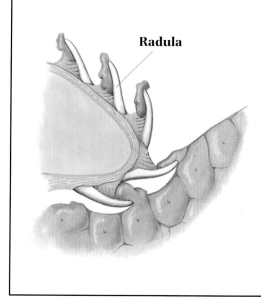

Radula

All teeth

Snails and slugs do not have to go to the dentist. They do lose teeth all the time, though, as they wear out their radula. This, however, is no problem as the teeth are replaced a bit like those of a shark by new teeth forming at the other end of the production line.

The actual pattern of these teeth varies and is a good way of telling tricky-to-identify species apart. One way of getting another imprint of a slug or snail's radula is to get a roll of camera film. Pull it out of the cartridge so that it is all over exposed and cloudy. Wet it and place it in a tub with some hungry slugs or snails. If you leave this overnight and investigate the film in the morning, you will be able to see tooth marks where the snail has chewed away at the emulsion. Place the film over a torch and view the marks through a magnifying lens to see them in more detail.

Above: *When inactive during either dry weather or in the winter, common Garden snails cluster together in sheltered places. If you were to prise one away, you would find its shell sealed shut with a tough, papery, waterproof cover.*

Experiment: Slime surfing

You will need:
• *small piece of clear glass or Perspex*
• *a slug or snail*
• *misting spray of water*
• *magnifying hand lens*

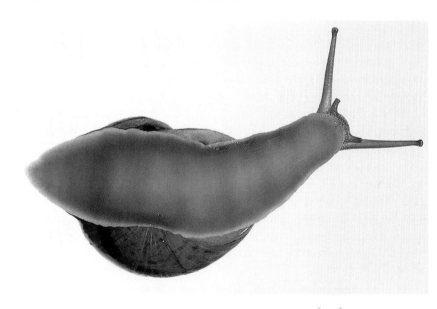

Below: *Underside of snail. Put your foot on it! Both slugs and snails can be persuaded to reveal their slippery secrets by placing them on a sheet of glass. Look for the dark bands of moving muscle.*

Both slugs and snails produce 'slime', a trail of mucous often visible as a silvery trail on walls and patios. This slime enables these animals to get about efficiently even without any legs!

Take a snail or a slug – it doesn't matter which. If you are not too keen to touch them with your finger you can use a couple of spoons to pick up most species and avoid getting sticky fingers. Place your chosen animal onto the piece of horizontal Perspex or glass and wait for it to start moving.

This sounds easier than it actually is. If your gastropod continues to be stubborn and refuses to emerge from its shell, or even shake a tentacle after a few minutes, it is time for you to get persuasive!

Most slugs and snails behave like this when the air is too dry for them – it's a survival instinct. You can reassure them that conditions are good by

Right: *One of the most noticeable snails are the Banded snails. The White-lipped and Brown-lipped snails are variable; they can be banded dark brown or black on yellow, the bands can be missing altogether or can be brown!*

lightly spraying them with water. (Run your fingers through a wet nail brush to produce a fine mist of water.)

When your mollusc is up and running gently lift up the clear sheet and watch your animal from below. What you should see is what looks like a conveyer belt effect of dark and light bands moving along the underside of the foot, called a sole. These are bands of muscles, the dark ones are raised and 'stepping' forward, the pale bands are in contact with the surface. But this would still not work if it wasn't for the famous secret ingredient – slime. Glands on the underside of the snail produce copious quantities of this stuff, which lubricates the ground and allows the mollusc almost to surf along though the garden.

On the trail of your snails

Have you ever had a slug or snail that lives in your house? Every night, when the heating has gone off, your gastropod guest emerges and goes wandering, leaving a wiggly trail on your carpet for you to find next morning! Although it looks like this animal moves around at random, there is a pattern to its activity. Forget the slug or snail that is lurking in your home though, because in my experience they are nearly impossible to see, unless you are prepared to wait around at night with a torch at the ready to catch the impostor red-handed (or should that be red-footed?).

Instead turn to your backyard, garden or park. The first bit of this experiment needs you to be a top tracker. You have to find a 'roost' of snails. Common Garden snails are the best, because they are big, darkish in colour and common! Look in all sorts of hidey holes; think about what a snail needs, i.e. shelter from predators and the sun. Look under piles of rocks and logs, walls, flower pots, overhanging plants, even ivy.

Once you have found your snails, make a note of where they are and then using enamel paint, mark each individual snail's shell with a number, making sure you do not get any paint on their soft parts.

Return the next day and see how many are still there. Mark any new ones. You can even look for other daytime hide-outs in the same garden or park and mark these with another colour. Do the snails mix up or do they return to the same place? If you do this well, soon you will know all the snails in your own patch personally, where they live and how many there are. If you are really keen, you can go out at night with a torch and look for them, plotting their positions on a map. Soon you will know how far they travel during the night!

Experiment: Watch 'em chomp!

There are lots of different ways of actually seeing a slug or snail's eating utensils or radula, but you will need a good magnifying lens and their complete co-operation to see their 'dentures' properly!

You can watch pond snails as they cling to the underside of the water surface, graze the film of microscopic plants, or pop one in a jam jar and watch it slide and sometimes chomp its way up the side of the glass.

But taking this last idea a little further you should be able to see this clearest of all with our old friend the common Garden snail. Not only has it got a big mouth, it will eat almost anything!

You will need:
- *food processor*
- *lettuce or grass or corn starch*
- *cuttlefish bone*
- *small piece of Perspex or glass*
- *paint brush*
- *snail*

First of all you need to tempt your snail to eat. Despite the fact that Garden snails seem to make short work of anything that is green in the garden, they can be fussy. You need to make a tasty soup – feel free to experiment! I've tried lettuce, which works well. Place the lettuce in the blender and turn it into a runny green liquid, add a bit of water, add a bit of chalk in the form of cuttle bone – snails need this for their shells.

Field Guide to common slugs and snails

Brown-lipped snail

A couple of common stripy snails that can also come in such plain guises as lemon yellow or plain brown just to confuse things. The two species, White-lipped and Brown-lipped, can be separated by the colour of the lip of the shell in adult specimens.

Garden snail

This is a very common snail just about everywhere. Its large size is second only to the rare Roman snail and its equally large appetite combined with its habit of hanging around gardens make it public enemy number one in the garden. Still, it is a beautiful snail to anyone prepared to look at it the right way.

Door snail

Not all terrestrial snails have a globular shell. Many, like the Door snail, so called because of a 'door like' mechanism that shuts the shell, have a very intricate corkscrew swirl to their shells. Look for these small snails under rocks, on old walls and among moss.

Hairy snail

Yes, snails come in highly strokeable forms too. There are several species that have this 'fluff' on their shells either as young or all through their lives – just do not ask me what it is for!

Strawberry snail

This is a very common snail and because of its small size and penchant for hanging out in and around the vegetable plot, greenhouse and herbaceous border it gets spread all over the place by humans.

Using the paint brush, paint this thin liquid onto one side of the clear Perspex or glass sheet, and leave it to dry. Repeat this a couple of times to build up a thick layer.

The next step is to place your hungry snail onto the horizontal surface, until it starts to move. (Use the water spray trick if your snail seems a little reluctant, see *Slime surfing* page 34, for details). Then slowly lift the sheet into a vertical position.

With your magnifying lens, you should notice your snail is hunched up and is not moving too fast. Instead it will be using its radula like sandpaper to scrape the dried soup from the surface of the sheet. You can see this action as the snail repeatedly opens its mouth, protrudes its radula and swallows. The snail will leave a distinctive feeding trail and you will see the zig zag marking left by the rows of teeth on the radula – this is a pattern that you often see on the glass of greenhouses where the algae has been grazed off by nocturnal slugs and snails.

Have a heart
If you grow pond snails in a small aquarium or tub that is kept under bright light and make sure they are fed well, they tend to grow quickly. When they do this their shells tend to develop a little on the thin side. This is handy for the snail enthusiast. Use a magnifying lens to see into the shell of a living snail and you will notice the mantle cavity and beating away next to it the two chambers of the heart.

Great pond snail
In areas of hard water, this is the commonest of the water snails in ponds, ditches and lakes. These aquatic 'mowers' of algae and weed, lay their eggs in jellied masses best found under the leaves of lily pads.

Ramshorn snail
One of a large group of flattened molluscs with shells, which look a bit like the coiled horns of male sheep. These come in two forms; both contain red blood a bit like ours, but one form has a dark pigment that masks this, while another seems to lack this pigment and has a body and foot that is quite literally 'blood red'.

Shelled slug
Although quite common, this animal is rarely seen, spending most of its time underground chasing its main prey, worms and other slugs. This anaemic-looking predator is also living proof that the difference between slugs and snails is pretty much an artificial one as this one has a little shell on its posterior.

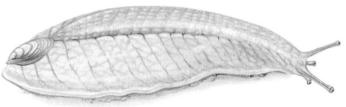

Great black slug
One of my favourites, a handsome beast in a glossy black livery, but it also comes in a bright orange form. It is also one of our biggest land molluscs, at full stretch reaching a good 15 cm in length. Give it a fright and it will contract presenting their leathery hide (not quite a shell, but not a bad effort all the same), produce lots of slime and rock gently from side to side.

Arthropods, Starting with Woodlice

All the creatures in this book are invertebrates – animals without a back bone. Up until now, all the animals mentioned – worms, slugs and snails – did not have legs. From now on in the book all the animals belong to an invertebrate category known as *Arthropods* meaning jointed legs. Have a quick flick through the rest of the book and every animal after this point has 'em.

Suits of armour

Whether it is a woodlouse, a butterfly or a springtail, all have legs and bodies that are made up of hard crunchy bits on the outside for at least part of their lifecycle. They need joints to move about. A good way to think of the Arthropods are animals in suits of armour!

There is a problem with suits of armour though. Imagine wearing one all the time – as you grew up, the suit of armour would get tighter and tighter and would eventually start to rub and hurt you. If you kept it on, you would end up permanently damaged and deformed. Arthropods have the same problem but they get over this in the same way that you would – they climb out of their suit and get one the next size up that will fit better.

The clever bit is that they have already got a soft suit underneath their old one. It's a bit baggy to start with but after it is pumped full of blood and air, it soon hardens into a brand new suit of armour.

So why have a suit of armour? Well, these animals are invertebrates; they have no backbone and no skeleton whatsoever inside their bodies. But arthropods have got a skeleton on the outside. Their bodies are in a container called an exoskeleton.

Above: *Cyclops. Stare into the murk of a pond for long enough and you will see these common little crustaceans 'flicking' around. They are named after the mythological beast and you can often see their single eye. This individual is a female carrying egg sacs.*

In the same way that our skeleton provides places to attach muscles and tendons, so it is with arthropods, just inside out!

The advantages of having your skeleton on the outside are many. Think back to the snail's shell. The shell gave protection from enemies, just like a suit of armour. Many arthropods have specially tough exoskeletons, some with knobbles, spikes and barbs on as extra protection and defence.

Mini robots

With a bit of added wax and oil a skeleton can be waterproof on the outside too. This doesn't mean that the animal stays dry – quite the opposite – a waterproof skin keeps water in, which means the animal can live in dry and hot places.

You can also add on lots of useful gadgets – things to make you go fast like a spring-tail's spring, extra sensors like eyes, a beetle's mouthparts and even wings. In fact you can think of them as little robots with lots of accessories for their own way of life.

The big disadvantage is that in between suits, when they climb out of their old skeleton to inflate their new one in order to grow, they go through a difficult patch. With a soft skeleton waiting to harden, arthropods become vulnerable to both predators and to the elements.

Woodlice – second cousin three times removed ... the crab

How many legs? Count them again – yep! definitely seven pairs. We all know these animals by name, but they have too many legs to be insects and not enough to be a millipede or centipede. So what are these strange little beasts?

Identical legs

Scientists have placed woodlice in a group called the *Isopods*, which means 'identical legs'. If you care to look, you will find that all of the walking legs are about the same length and pretty much identical.

Isopods belong to an even bigger class of animals you will be much more familiar with down by the side of the sea, the *Crustaceans*, which include, among many other strange and odd-looking beasts, lobsters, crabs and shrimps!

In fact in an evolutionary sense woodlice have really only just stepped onto the land; most of the isopods still live in water. Woodlice are one step ahead of their brothers in half-shells and you can see why if you catch one, and gently flip the little chap over to investigate its belly. As well as seven pairs of walking legs all scrabbling to get the right way up again, you will see towards the back end after the last pair of walking legs, a small area of what look at first glance to be pale scales.

These are gills. Contained here is the technology that was the secret to the woodlouse's successful conquering of dry land. By having an insight into how they work, it means you will understand a lot more about the ways woodlice live their lives.

If you care to examine some of the other members of the crustacean club that have not yet left the water and have exposed gills, like prawns, freshwater shrimps and

Above: *When looking for woodlice, walls and rockeries are ideal hunting grounds, but put stones back where you found them. Two reasons: they are the homes of these animals, and if you don't, you may not be very popular with the rest of your household.*

Above: *Moulting woodlouse. As arthropods grow they shed their suit of armour for a new one underneath. Woodlice moult in two stages, losing the back end before the front.*

Moulting

Most other arthropods shed their suit of armour all at once, but woodlice do it in two stages. The back end comes off first and the new exoskeleton is left to harden, then the front end is moulted. If you discover woodlice mid-moult they do look a little odd. The soft bit is always a pale, almost white, colour, giving you a two-tone woodlouse. The colour, shape and texture of these plates are the best way to tell most species of woodlice apart.

even an animal that is pretty much a wet woodlouse, the Water louse (see *Nearest and dearest – the woodlouse's garden relatives* on page 45), and look under their rear end, you will see these gills in action. Look back at a woodlouse again and the structures are still there – they are just not flapping about.

A woodlouse's plates are thin; think of them as flattened legs, folded back on themselves at the knee. Use a magnifying lens of x15 or more and you can see water sloshing about between the plates. So even these little armoured tanks that have invaded the land are using the same gills as their mates living in water. Woodlice must keep their gills wet for them to work properly and this is one of the reasons woodlice are found only in wet and damp places – they need water to breathe!

Hard armour
Woodlice bodies are protected by lots of tough plates that overlap each other. These plates are physically very hard because they are built with calcium carbonate, which is basically chalk. They are not, however, very waterproof, so woodlice if caught out in the dry lose water very quickly. Some species, such as the Pill wood-

The Woodlouse a.k.a. ...

'Grammazows', 'chiggy pigs', 'fairies pigs', 'cheeselogs', 'pissibeds', 'bibblebugs', 'coffin cutters', 'Gods pigs', 'cudworms' and 'pill bugs' are all names that are or have been used to describe woodlice. According to a study by Dr Walter Collinge of York Museum in the 1930s, these little creatures have over 65 colloquial names! All these names bear testimony to an animal that is not only instantly recognisable by most people but has been trundling in and out of our lives since time began.

louse, survive better than others in dry habitats because they have covered their plates with a waxy layer that stops water passing out of their bodies.

Brood pouch
Flip a few woodlice over and inspect their undersides. Sometimes you can come across a female with a brood pouch between her front legs. The brood patch sometimes looks white or yellow and it is here that the eggs

Body design

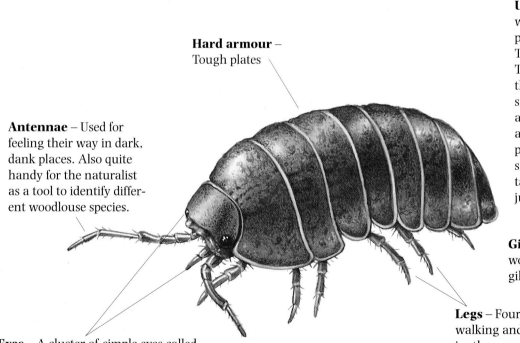

Uropods – At the back end a woodlouse has four little pointy bits that stick out. These are called uropods. There are actually two but they fork to give the impression of four. They act like antennae for the back end, and some even give off nasty pungent chemicals to deter sneaky predators that try to take them by surprise and jump them from behind.

Hard armour – Tough plates

Antennae – Used for feeling their way in dark, dank places. Also quite handy for the naturalist as a tool to identify different woodlouse species.

Gills – Get close and turn a woodlouse over and you'll see gills at the back end.

Legs – Fourteen legs are used for walking and at the back of their bodies there are an extra ten special, flattened legs used for breathing.

Eyes – A cluster of simple eyes called *ocelli* are found in most species on either side of the head. Not much use for distinguishing anything but light and dark.

Gills and how they work

In their simplest form gills are a way to breathe for animals that live in water. Fish have them, tadpoles have them, crabs have them and so do many aquatic insect nymphs.

Here is the magnified underside back end of a woodlouse. The gills are structures designed to absorb oxygen from the water and put it into the animals bloodstream at the same time getting rid of waste gases. To move these gases about more efficiently, it helps if the skin covering the gills is thin and if blood flows as close to the surface as possible. This is why if you look at gills in other animals, they are often transparent. In animals with red blood, such as fish and tadpoles, they look red (you can see the blood through the skin). Such animals often flap or wave their gills about to speed up the flow of water and gases over the gill structures (in a similar way that a fan speeds up the flow of fresh air around a room). That is, basically, gills for you, and they have to be wet to work properly!

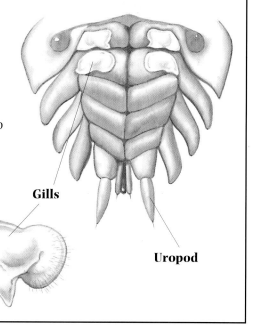

Gills

Uropod

are kept until they hatch out into a pool of liquid. The babies remain in this pouch until they are big enough to survive in the outside world.

Hide and seek
Woodlice can be found in all kinds of places but because they are nocturnal (active at night) you must look for them in their hideouts during the day. You do not have to look very hard. I used to get into trouble with my mum over these animals as I was always disturbing her rockery to find them. But you do not have to destroy the garden to turn up at least a few. Pretty

much any object, be it a log, stone, brick or bit of old tin will offer shelter to these animals, which are lovers of the damp and the dark.

Group addiction
Even though their body design is pretty much the same, forage around for long enough and you will soon notice that there are lots of different looking woodlice. Some are separable only by the number of segments in their antennae, others have a completely different colour or texture. In fact once you have noticed this you will find this group of animals rather addictive.

Below: *Evolutionarily speaking, woodlice have only just stepped out of the water and share many crustacean features in common with their aquatic relatives like the Water louse; they even have gills.*

Below: *Woodlice lying low. Woodlice often cluster in dank dark places, hiding out from their worst enemy, the dry! They can't tolerate dry conditions for long; they still need water to live and breathe.*

Above: *The sight of one of these creatures scuttling across the shagpile is enough to send many home owners into a panic. Visions of the house rotting into a damp woodlouse-infested mush soon follow.*

I sentence you to 'death by vacuum cleaner'!

Nowadays we commonly think of woodlice as pests. But in the past they have been revered and put on a pedestal of respect. So next time you are about to commit a house-wandering woodlouse to almost certain death by vacuum cleaner think about some of this stuff.

Woodlice have appeared in many famous works of art from paintings to poetry. Historically, they have been eaten by humans and used as medicine to cure various stomach complaints from indigestion and ulcers to tuberculosis. They were given to cows to help them chew the cud, hence one of their names 'cudworm'.

In case of emergency they were often worn around the neck in a little locket to be taken when troubles arose, like a kind of primitive indigestion tablet!

Why are woodlice considered pests? Well, to be quite honest with you, all I can come up with is because they are creepy-crawlies and we do not understand them. Woodlice do not do any harm, even those of us who are plagued by them trundling across our carpets have only our buildings to blame! The woodlice are there because there is either a hole for them to crawl through from outside or your house is damp, and when a home is damp woodlice feel at home too.

It may also be this habit of living in damp buildings that has given them the reputation of being unlucky, which I guess they are, if this means forking out for new double glazing or a damp course for your home!

Recycling

Woodlice rarely eat living plants, they sometimes have a nibble at particularly succulent and tender seedlings but nothing serious. Most of a woodlouse's menu consists of dead or rotten material and they will also graze algae and have a munch of fungi too. However, they do more good than harm in the grand scheme of things; they play an important role in the world of composting, breaking down bits of dead plant in our compost heaps and in a natural setting, recycling dead wood and leaf litter into the soil.

Experiment: Stinky pigs

In this little demonstration you can learn a little about woodlice biology, their social life and how they got their German name of 'pissibeds'!

You will need:
• *small jam jar with lid*
• *some leaves and bark*
• *damp soil*
• *selection of woodlice*

First make a nice little home for your woodlice. Place damp soil and a few leaves and bark into your jar.

Pop in your woodlice and put the lid on. Leave them for a couple of days, making sure you keep them in a cool dark place. There will be enough air in the jar to last them for some time.

Then after a few days, quickly remove the lid and take a big sniff from the jar. Pheweee! What a pong! It smells of wee.

Now you know how they get the name of 'pissibeds' in Germany. The reason they smell is that they do not pee like you and me. They actually excrete the chemical ammonia – one of the waste products of living – as a gas through their skins! It is this you can smell as soon as you lift the jar lid.

This distinct smell may also be a reason why you often find woodlice clustered together, they prefer the distinct perfume of their friends and the place they live, a clever idea but not quite home sweet home!

Set your woodlice free when you've finished.

Experiment: Give 'em a choice

The things that control a woodlouse's movements more than anything are light and humidity (the amount of moisture in the air). Woodlice keep moving if things do not feel too comfortable. This is why if you see a wood-louse out of cover on a sunny day, it simply keeps on walking. They walk until they find the conditions they like, then when it starts to feel right they make more and more turns until they find the perfect habitat and then simply stop.

Here are a couple of simple experiments that allow you to find out exactly what makes a woodlouse tick and why you find them where you do. *See panel below.*

You will need:
• *Board 30 cm x 30 cm*
• *Plasticine*
• *sheet of Perspex 30 cm x 30 cm*
• *black card or paper*
• *cotton wool*
• *water*
• *water-based marker pen*

Experiment 1: Wet or Dry?
Place a piece of damp cotton wool in one side of the arena and put five woodlice in each compartment. Watch and see where the woodlice end up after a couple of hours. Do they like it moist or dry?

Making your woodlice experiment

1 Place your board, which should be the same size as the sheet of Perspex (30 cm x 30 cm), onto a table or a flat surface.
2 Roll out your plasticine to form long sausage shapes and make a wall on the board that goes all around the edges to form a perimeter. This is your arena for your woodlouse experiment.
3 Now divide the arena with another three smaller strips of plasticine of the same dimensions, leaving two small gaps.
4 Now place your perspex on top. The idea is that when you place the perspex on top like a roof, you will have a sealed woodlouse-proof arena, with two chambers. The woodlice can move between them via the two small gaps.
5 Now follow the two experiments as described above.

You can add another dimension to this experiment by repeating it with one woodlouse or if you are doing this with a friend, two woodlice. You place both your woodlice in the dry side without the damp cotton wool. Then after picking which woodlouse belongs to whom, using your marker pens, or Chinagraph pencils, follow your woodlouse, tracing its movements with the pen.

When it steps into the damp and humid side of the choice chamber, what happens to its movements?

Experiment 2: Light or Dark?
Remove the damp cotton wool. This time cover one of the compartments with black card or paper and place five woodlice in each compartment, before putting the Perspex roof on the whole arena. Return after a couple of hours. Where are all the woodlice now?

Weird friends, cool enemies!

Woodlice are quite long-lived and they can live to the ripe old age of four, meaning they have the same kind of life expectancy as a gerbil! However, it isn't exactly a stress-free existence for them in the woodlouse world.

Despite all their tank-like armour and the nasty secretions produced by their bodies for defence purposes, woodlice are prey to many creatures. It is surprising

Field guide to common woodlice

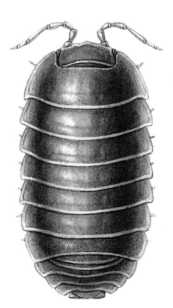

Pill woodlouse
Also called pill bugs, these woodlice are often found at the base of walls. They roll themselves into a 'pill', or ball, if you disturb them.

Porcellio scaber
Another very common woodlouse to find in your garden. Covered in pale spots, this woodlouse hangs out under stones or logs, but may go higher up in trees too.

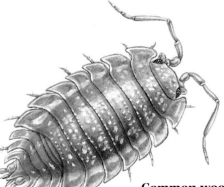

Androniscus dentiger
This woodlouse is 6mm long only and very pale. It lives in your compost heap, cellar or leaf litter.

Common woodlouse
This one looks flatter than other woodlice. As its name suggests, this is very common in the garden in clusters under stones, logs and bark.

how many are partial to a *Porcellio* (woodlouse) from time to time.

Apparently 40% of all woodlice are eaten by centipedes, whose sharp, sickle-like jaws can make short work of an armour-plated louse.

Shrews and Hedgehogs will put 'em away given half a chance and toads have been reared almost entirely on a diet of woodlice with no apparent ill effects.

There are a few specialist 'hit creatures' that will prey entirely on these unfortunate crustaceans. They present particularly unpleasant ways to go. How would you choose between death by *Dysdera* the spider (page 62) and being eaten alive by the maggots of a parasitic fly?

37 varieties

There are about 37 different kind of woodlouse found in the British Isles today. Some 30 or so are native, the rest have been introduced from abroad.

If you want to encourage these little suits of armour into your garden, go and get some dead wood and make a log pile in a corner. The most important thing is to leave the wood alone; if you expose them too often they will move on.

Nearest and dearest – the woodlouse's garden relatives

Freshwater shrimp
Stir up the silty soup at the bottom of any pond or ditch and you will see many of these guys scarper. They are scavengers and perform the same jobs as woodlice do above the surface.

Cyclops
With its single eye, the Cyclops looks even more alien than its crustacean relatives. The females carry the eggs in clusters like large panniers on their sides.

Water flea
A beam of sunlight filtering into the surface water of a pond during the summer will often illuminate countless thousands of these tiny crustaceans jiggling around. It's jiggling to us, to them it's filtering microscopic plankton from the water, finding mates and simply trying to stay near the surface.

Water louse
So very nearly a woodlouse, these aquatic animals are very recognisable as the closest relatives of the woodlouse. Like their terrestrial cousins and the Freshwater shrimps they are recyclers, grubbing around in the weed and dead plant matter at the bottom of ponds.

Centipedes and Millipedes – Loads of Legs

These are two groups of animals with lots and lots of legs, but not as many as their names suggest. Millipedes do not have thousands of legs and centipedes certainly do not have hundreds. If you do not believe me, try counting them! Both centipedes and millipedes are often lumped together as *Myriapods* and it will come as no surprise to hear that this literally translates to 'many legs'!

Above: *Get into the habit of lifting stones, digging in the soil or looking under bark and finding centipedes and millipedes shouldn't be a problem.*

A wealth of walking gear

However many legs they really have, it is this undeniable abundance of walking gear that makes centipedes and millipedes stand out from the rest of the creepy-crawlies.

World record

The world record for legs belongs to a millipede with 750.

First things first though, millipedes and centipedes are not closely related at all. They are like chalk and cheese, similar body designs, but used for completely different purposes.

Frantic centipedes

There are many different species of centipede, some are longer than others, some are pale or white, others a rich red to green. But things they have in common are that they are all carnivores, predators eating other small creatures in the soil or leaf litter. If you were small and lived under logs, you can bet that centipedes would be the stuff of your worst nightmares.

For a start, they are fast. Like a Cheetah, centipedes use their lanky legs combined with a long thin body to chase down their quarry, even when it runs and tries to hide in a nook or cranny. This is helped by a very distinctive profile; if you look at a centipede face on, you will notice it is flat, perfect for fitting under things.

All these qualities make centipedes very easy to recognise so if you find an animal with lots of legs, which then wakes up and starts sprinting around, you can be sure you've got yourself a centipede! Centipedes have long legs – some have a hundred and some have fewer; it depends on the species. But long legs are useful for sprinting around in pursuit of dinner.

Pinchers and feelers
What makes centipedes particularly effective as predators is their hardware, the cutlery with which they bite. Or should I say 'pinch' because that is what they really do. If you look at the front end of a large centipede you will be able to see that it has two evil-looking claws

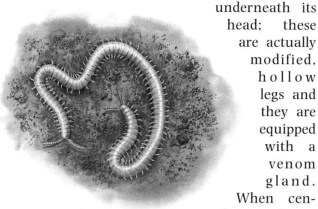

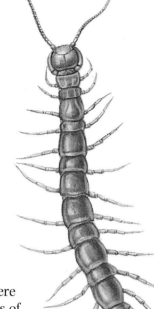

underneath its head; these are actually modified, hollow legs and they are equipped with a venom gland. When centipedes catch up with their prey they give it a quick nip with these modified legs and inject the venom into them, which quickly overpowers and kills even the most energetic of woodlice.

Use your bug restrainer and if you manage to slow down a centipede long enough to study it under a hand magnifying lens, something I strongly recommend as they are truly awesome animals, you should try looking for their eyes. You should spot the tiny little simple eyes found on some species, positioned low down on the side of the head capsule. Obviously, to the invertebrate expert, these eyes cannot be used much for seeing things with, so how does a centipede catch its prey and get around – especially in the dark world of the life under the litter?

Well, the clue is in the question. It is so dark, light only penetrates their world when we lift the lid on their home, centipedes don't actually need eyes. Instead they get around in the same way we do if we are blindfolded – they feel.

Look at a centipede; because it can move so fast, faster than a millipede, it needs to be even better at feeling its way around. That is why they have a splendid set of antennae on their head. These are very sensitive to vibration and touch and probably to smell too. But as if this isn't enough, at the very tip of the other end of their body, they have modified legs, which act as feelers too. In addition, to a point, every one of the legs is sensitive. With all these sensors it is no wonder that centipedes are so highly strung, a fact that becomes apparent if you've tried to catch one and put it in the bug restrainer!

Left: Haplophilus subterraneus *is a soil-living centipede, with more than 80 pairs of legs and a pale head.*

Right: *Just compare this Common centipede with the Snake millipede at the foot of the page. It has fewer legs, a fast and active disposition – qualities of a predator.*

Mooching millipedes

As with centipedes, there are many different kinds of millipede, but where they can get a little tricky is that there are some which look a little bit like centipedes. But I won't confuse you yet and I'll talk about this later.

What shapes a millipede's life is that it feeds on very different stuff. In fact, millipedes are mostly vegetarians! Some scavenge, but none of them actually feed on living animals. And because plants and dead things do not move very fast, neither does a millipede have to.

Compared with centipedes they are very chilled out animals, at best managing not much more than an amble, usually to get out of the bright light.

Smooth operator
Their body shape is generally very different from that of a centipede, most have a chunky, tall profile with a body shaped a bit like a hose pipe, with short legs attached underneath – four per segment.

The strong, smooth, long body means that like a tube train, millipedes can fit into narrow crevices in the soil and litter and because they feed on dead material and not living things they need to be able to go places no

Left: *Snake millipede – Millipedes live life at a much more lethargic pace. For a start the dead plants that they feed on do not move very fast and they do not have many predators because they have a chemical defence system.*

Masquerading millipedes

Some millipedes look a little bit like centipedes. These are the *Polydesmids* (see *Field guide* section). They have flat plates which stick out on either side of their bodies, but just like other millipedes, they are slow-moving, have short antennae and have their legs underneath their bodies.

other animals have gone. They need to be able to barge their way through and that is why they have so many legs; with them they can generate a huge pushing force. (Try holding a millipede in a clenched fist and you will feel how strong it is as it tries to push its way between your fingers.) Because they do not have big flouncy feelers (they actually tuck their head under when they walk!) and long sticking out legs like a centipede they have nothing that is likely to get caught up on things!

Like centipedes, they have poor eyesight, but they do not need huge feelers because their food doesn't run around and they don't move very fast. They can make do with having a set of short antennae on the head.

Millipedes have two pairs of short legs per segment giving tremendous pushing power but slow travel time.

Lots of segments

Both animals have a body that is made up of joints and, like a bicycle chain, this means they can have a tough outer skeleton and all its advantages, plus the flexibility of a worm, allowing them to move easily among leaf litter and soil.

Different body work

There are around fifty different kinds of millipede in the British Isles and some of them can be a bit of a challenge to identify, They do, however, fall into three main categories (see *Field guide* section).

Body design

Centipede head – Because of their fast pace of life they are bristling with sensory equipment to help them cope. Centipedes have a flat profile for slipping into crevices and between the leaf litter.

Millipede – Compared with the centipede these are slow and sluggish, designed to push through soil and litter. They have a strong and powerful profile. Millipedes are tube-shaped.

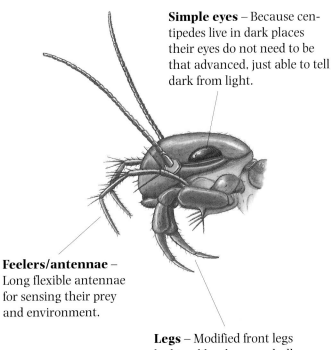

Simple eyes – Because centipedes live in dark places their eyes do not need to be that advanced, just able to tell dark from light.

Feelers/antennae – Long flexible antennae for sensing their prey and environment.

Legs – Modified front legs looking like claws are hollow and designed to mash and inject venom into prey.

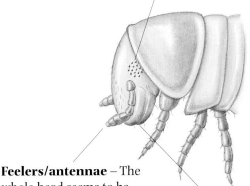

Simple eyes – The eyes of a millipede are even more basic, clusters of simple eyes set low on the head, just enough to detect the difference between light and dark.

Feelers/antennae – The whole head seems to be hunched up and looking towards its boots. Its antennae are short and small and seem simply to touch and stroke the ground in front of the millipede's head, tasting and touching all the time.

Mouthparts – these are strong and sturdy, for chomping through dead plant material.

Field guide to common centipedes and millipedes

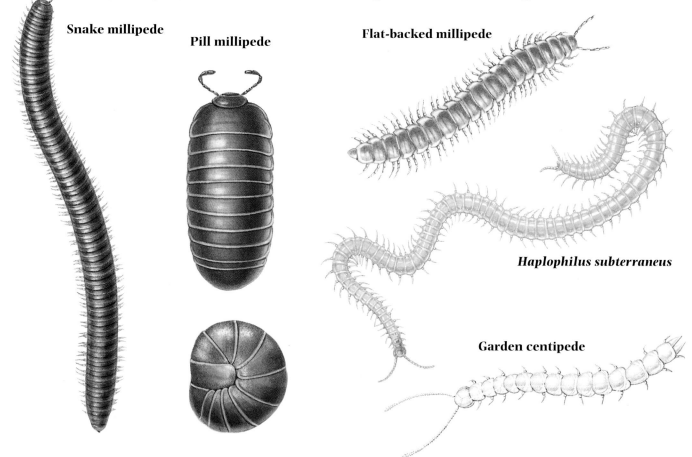

Snake millipede

Pill millipede

Flat-backed millipede

Haplophilus subterraneus

Garden centipede

Snake millipedes

These are the ones that are usually black and are very common in and around the garden. They are usually black or brown and there is at least one very pale species, the Spotted snake millipede. They all have a round profile, like a vacuum cleaner hose, and they will coil up like a watch spring when disturbed. To defend themselves further they have glands along the side of their body (these show up as the bright spots along the side of the Spotted snake millipede), which produce really nasty liquid chemicals, including cyanide, making them very unpleasant to eat. (They are not dangerous to humans and this defensive fluid will merely stain our hands.)

Pill millipedes

These are like a shorter version of the above and are often mistaken for the similar-looking Pill woodlouse (see page 44). Look underneath at their legs for confirmation; a Pill millipede has loads more than the fourteen of the woodlouse. Because they can curl up into a neat tight ball, hence their name, they are very good at avoiding desiccation and can cope with much drier conditions than the other millipedes.

Flat-backed millipedes

Also known as *Polydesmids*, these are really tube-shaped millipedes with shield-like extensions sticking out either side of their body. They defend themselves with chemicals and you can sometimes catch the whiff of almonds, especially if you have had one captive in a small pot. This is the distinctive smell of cyanide.

Centipedes

Of the 50 or so centipede species that live in Britain, all belong to two basic body designs. Over half are a job to see unless you dig around in the soil. These are the *Geophilomorphs* and they are long and stringy and live in the soil. They are very narrow, but also have very long bodies enabling them to move easily in among particles of soil. They are so flexible, they can double back on themselves and even tie their own bodies in knots. In fact often when you dig them up they are in this tied-up position. Most of these soil-dwelling centipedes are a listless, anaemic-looking yellow or white.

The other shape that centipedes come in is the flat form that lives under stones and logs and among the leaf litter. These have fewer legs than the soil-dwellers, but are much bigger, bolder, obvious creatures.

Arachnids – Things with Eight Legs!

Let's get this straight – anything with more than six legs is not an insect, and that includes all of the animals in this group. *Arachnids* comprise an order of mini-beasts that include the spiders and a few other oddballs. They come in a variety of shapes and sizes but the two things they all have in common is four pairs of walking legs and no antennae.

Above: *You can look for spiders almost anywhere – this garden wall was a web of activity!*

Right: *Probably the most infamous of British arachnids, the House spider is rarely seen sitting still, more likely running for refuge behind the sofa.*

Spiders

These are the most commonly encountered arachnids around the garden and unfortunately they have a bit of a public relations problem. At times it seems the whole world is suffering from what I call 'Miss Muffet syndrome' or Arachnophobia. It's a troublesome fact of life but all you have to do is just mention the word 'spider', let alone reveal a living one, and you are pretty much guaranteed to send someone flying out of the room in hysterics!

Yet, even the biggest British spider is thousands of times smaller than a human. Although all spiders use venom to subdue their prey and a few can just about

manage to sink a fang through our leathery skin, there is no real excuse to fear any British spider. None can cause us any harm and for every reason we give for placing them under the foot there are a thousand good reasons to like them too.

Spiders come in many shapes and sizes. You get gangly ones, dumpy ones, fat ones and thin ones; some are very hairy, others appear smooth as silk, some are sombre in colour and others, yes believe it or not, are actually quite pretty! If there is a habitat to be lived in you can bet there will be a spider of some sort living in it! There are spiders that hunt alone, spiders that spin elaborate traps, underwater spiders, surfing spiders,

Body design

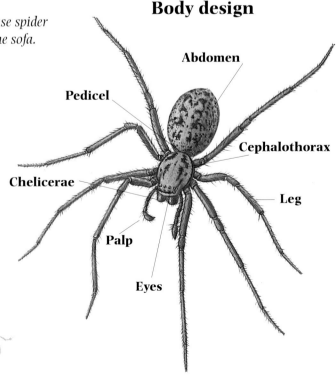

parachuting spiders, spiders that jump, spiders that steal from other spiders and even pirate spiders that murder their fellows. They are a truly versatile bunch. But no matter how different the 620 British species all look from each other, they do have a number of things in common.

Know your way around a spider

Spiders come in two halves joined by a narrow waist called a pedicel. You can see this much with the naked eye, but for a more thorough examination, you will need to use a hand lens and it will also help to use a bug restrainer (see page 14) for some of the faster ones.

The front bit is a bit like the head and thorax of an insect combined. Its technical name is cephalothorax, which sounds complicated until you realise it means 'head chest'.

The cephalothorax can be thought of as the engine room and control centre of a spider. It contains a lot of the nervous system and muscles to power those infamously gangly eight legs, the stomach and its own powerful muscles, the venom glands as well as other bits and pieces. All these trappings are encased in a box-like external skeleton, with a hard shield on top.

Eyes

If you cast your magnifying lens to the front of the spider, you should see the beady little black eyes that appear to be staring back at you! Unless you are looking at a jumping spider, some of which can see detail at a distance of 30 cm, the chances are that this is just a figment of your imagination because the eyes of spiders are so simple that most cannot see very well at all. However, they are far from blind and some definitely can use their eyes to detect mates and predators by seeing detail and movement. Some wolf spiders use light to navigate by and all spiders' eyes can at least detect differences in light and dark.

Most species have eight eyes arranged in two rows but there are always exceptions to the rules – some have six (have a look at a Woodlouse spider) and some have only four, others have a large growth that looks for all the world like the post office tower with eyes placed directly on top of the spider's head. Depending on the type of spider, the arrangement of this bundle of 'seeing gear' is a very useful identification tool.

Tools of the trade

The 'mouth' of a spider is a set of appendages that process the unfortunate prey in different stages a bit like a factory conveyer belt. To see these things yourself is a

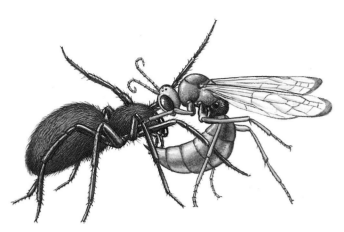

Above: *Spiders may be predators but that does not mean they are invincible – they have plenty of predators of their own. One of the nastiest ways to go if you are a spider is by the paralysing sting of a Spider-hunting wasp.*

little tricky – they tend to be hidden behind each other but look at a shed skin or flip your spider over in the bug restrainer so you can see its underside and I'll talk you through.

The fangs – or in technical talk, the chelicerae – are situated either side of the head. They come in two parts: the base, which are the obvious two bits below the spiders eyes if you look at it head on and the hard shiny sharp tip, which is often tucked under the spider. These are not only instruments of deathly dealings, but to the spider they are sometimes used in defence and are

Above: *Here's looking at you. Well, assuming you are within 20 cm or so. These are the eyeballs of a jumping spider and they are some of the best in the arthropod world.*

Diamonds in the dark

Go out at night with a hand torch and investigate your herbaceous border or simply catch a hunting spider and take it and a torch into the cupboard under the stairs. Shine the light into your spider's eyes and you will see they glow like red hot coals. The reason for this is due to a reflective layer, called a tapetum, in the back of the eye behind the retina. This is the part of the eye that contains all the light-sensitive cells. Normally light passes through the retina and is absorbed but in animals with a tapetum the light is bounced back through the retina a second time. This doubles the sensitivity of the eye to light.

really the nearest thing these animals have to hands – they use them to pick up material, wind up silk, dig burrows and carry their eggs around. Some of the tiny money spiders even use them to produce noises by rubbing them together!

The tip of the fang has a microscopic hole in it. This is where the venom, squeezed out of the muscular venom gland somewhere in the head region, is injected into the prey a bit like a hypodermic needle. Once delivered, the venom does two jobs – it paralyses the prey to stop it struggling and then it slowly dissolves the prey insect's insides, turning them into insect soup.

House spider

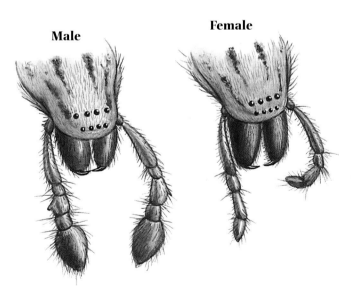

Male **Female**

Above: *Palps. He or she? Many male spiders have swollen tips to their palps, used in courtship displays and as sexual pipettes to inject sperm into the female!*

It is this juice that the spider feeds on and so it has to go about straining this off from the rest of the carnage in the same way we strain tea or jam. A spider's food filter is the several layers of hairs and bristles that protrude around the mouth. All the spider has to do is suck hard through its mouth (the small hole that is pointed to by the fangs of the spider when it is at rest).

And, boy! Can spiders suck! They have a very muscular stomach attached to inside walls of the cephalothorax. Imagine a flat bag a bit like the bladder on a pair of bellows – when you pull it open, air rushes in. What happens is that instead of air, the soup that has been made of the poor insect is slurped up into the mouth.

The famous eight

Everybody knows spiders have eight legs! So why when you count 'em do you keep coming up with ten? Well, the chances are you are also counting a pair of what look like legs that stick out either side of the head. These are palps, and besides being one segment shorter than a leg, they are definitely not used for walking. If you watch a spider going about its business you will see how it uses the palps to tap and touch things as it travels. You would use your arms and hands in the same way if you couldn't see very well, but your hands are just used for feeling. A spider's palps are super sensitive and are used to grab, feel and taste prey as well as playing a big role in the sex lives of male spiders (and, incidentally, a good way of telling adult males from females).

So the next time a House spider falls in your bath, impress your friends and family by being able to tell whether it is a Mr or Mrs Tegenaria domestica. Have a close look at its palps if it is a male (they usually are – it is the males that go 'walkies' looking for females and often end up falling foul of our porcelain bathroom fittings!), it will look as if it has boxing gloves on! These are used like 'sexual pipettes' to inject sperm into the female. Some species of wolf spider and zebra spider use them like flags to signal in a kind of spider semaphore either a threat or a chat up line – telling the female he quite fancies her and to make sure that she fancies him. If not, you see, he may end up as dinner – female spiders are bigger than males and if hungry or not in the mood for love they sometimes consume their suitor!

The actual walking legs are also multi-purpose. Each leg is covered in sensory hairs and pressure pads so that the spider uses them to walk and feel at the same time. They work by naturally being full of blood under high pressure and muscles pull the legs as they walk. The high pressure blood system is demonstrated indirectly when you see a dead spider.

Why are spiders hairy?

It may be what makes you go 'Urrgh!', but to a spider its hairy legs are more than just to make them look scary. Look very closely at the body surface and this is also covered in a pelage of tiny hairs. A bald spider would be a dead one as spiders need these bristles for all manner of tasks essential to their lives. To a spider its hairs are not so much a fur coat as its camouflage, ears, nose, grip, taste, comb and hairbrush! These are not just a bunch of bristles either, there are many different kinds cut out for different kinds of work.

Some of the short hairs that cover the body in a dense velvet are what gives the spiders their camouflage, patterns and sometimes groovy colours. The colours act to break up the spider's outline and help them blend into their background – just think how a Crab spider would get on if it stood out from its background, it wouldn't catch much dinner. If wolf spiders were anything but a nice mottled brown and grey, they would become everything in the gardens favourite snack. Other hairs are more like the sort of gadgets James Bond would have.

Fancy feet

It's hair that enables spiders to crawl up the smooth surfaces of walls and take a stroll across the ceiling. Each foot has a device made from lots of special hairs, called

Above: *Using the mesh of web in its labyrinth and the highly sensitive bristles and hairs on its body and legs, this Labyrinth spider has efficiently detected and despatched a victim, in this instance a cricket.*

scopula hairs (*scopa* means broom in Latin), each of which looks just like a brush as it is divided yet again into hundreds of even smaller extensions each with a flattened end, looking like a tiny bendy spade. What makes spiders 'stick' is that each 'spade' uses the surface tension of the microscopic film of water found on most objects – the principle is the same when a drink mat or coaster sticks to the bottom of a wet glass.

Even a spider with only a few of these scopulae on its foot, such as a crab spider which has 30 only, can achieve 160,000 separate grips on a surface.

This is why some species with even more scopulae than this are able to support more than ten times their own weight when resting on even the smoothest surface of glass!

Some of the other hairs on the feet, found nowhere else on the spiders' body, are sensitive to other things such as tastes and chemicals.

On the legs there are hairs used to comb the silk to produce the right texture and yet others are found there that are used as a hair brush to keep all the other hairs in good working order.

Webs

A hectare of field may have 5.5 million spider webs in autumn.

Vibrations

The talents of hair do not stop there! Spiders haven't got ears but they can hear in a way. They pick up vibrations and sound waves in the air which is pretty much what our ears do. Just about all the hairs and bristles scattered on their body have a nerve ending. It's these that give spiders a great 'sense of vibration'. They feel their environment with their whole body all the time.

You may notice that there are hairs and bristles of different thickness. The larger ones are mainly used as triggers to tell a spider that something is moving or not – if you try tickling one of these hairs of a spider with a pin, watch how it reacts. There are other hairs even more sensitive – these are the finer, feathery hairs called trichobothria. Because they are so fine and feathery they are easily 'blown' by even a tiny vibration or breeze and can tell a spider where its next meal is, quite literally, coming from.

Specialised purposes

Some specialised spiders have specialised hairs for specialised jobs. Water spiders for instance rely on the shape of hairs and bristles on their body to trap a layer of air in place, allowing them to breathe under water – so you could say its hairs are its scuba gear.

Wolf spiders are able to carry all their babies on their backs because their hairs are modified with a knob, which acts a bit like a handle or grip for their young to hold onto!

Breathing with books?

It is a well known fact, well at least it is in arachnological circles, that you can wear a spider out! This doesn't mean that we should all go around forcing them to sprint. Most of the time spiders are slow unless running from a predator or pouncing on prey, when of course speed is of the essence, but they cannot keep it up for very long. The reason for this is that they do not have the most efficient of lungs.

There are two ways in which spiders breathe. They have a special organ called a book lung – you cannot see it easily but you may just make out a tiny pair of slits on the underside of the abdomen, near the waist. Air passes into the spider here and within a cavity it wafts over lots of thin plates that look like the pages of a book – here oxygen passes to the spiders' blood and at the same time waste gases pass out.

More active spiders may also have a system similar to those of insects, a network of fine tubes that take air from outside, through a tiny hole in the body wall, called a spiracle, to the internal organs of the spider.

Spider vagabonds – wolf spiders

Walk through long grass in the summer and you may notice small spiders scatter from your path in huge numbers. There are so many of them and they are all over the place that the sheer quantity of spider life encourages you to take them for granted. Don't! Get down on your hands and knees and look at these spiders and you will notice a miracle in micro-mothering.

Most of these spiders will be wolf spiders. They are so called because they hunt like wolves. They use their big eyes to spot their prey and then they chase it down and pounce. They do not spin a web, and they certainly do not hunt in packs, although sometimes it may appear that way because there are so many of them! One of the commonest is a species called *Pardosa amentata*. Like many of the wolf spiders it is various shades of brown with a beige stripe running down its back, perfect camouflage for a hunter.

Because these spiders do not have a true home or web, the females have to carry their eggs around with them in a silken cocoon slung beneath her abdomen. It is this pale off-white pellet of silk that makes the females stand out during the height of summer. You will find that you will probably notice the off-white egg sac before you see the spider carrying it!

Now is the time to start spider watching in earnest, or you could keep one in a vivarium (see *Making your tegenarium*, page 60). What the observant will notice is that the females appear to change shape and look a little different – peer a little closer and you will see that they are now carrying a bundle of spiderlings on their backs. Wolf spiders are good mums and will carry their young

Below: *Spotted wolf spider. The female carries her eggs in a sac attached to her spinnerets.*

for about a week, giving them some protection from predators, a head start before they wander off into the grassy jungle on their own.

Feel the vibe

Many spiders do not go out on the prowl like wolf spiders, but at the same time they do not exactly build an architectural masterpiece like the orb spiders. Look on dry banks and especially walls with crumbly mortar and you will see the tiny burrows that show up white, being reinforced by a dense weave of silk. If you scrutinise even more you can probably make out the finer, almost invisible, radiating threads arranged like the spokes from a bicycle wheel hub. These are the secret to getting to meet the owner.

The spider spends the majority of its life waiting in the security of its hole and the only way to get him to answer the door is by giving him a buzz and tricking him into thinking you are dinner. There are a couple of ways of doing this. The first is handy if you happen to have a musician in the family. You need a tuning fork (you can get these from musical instrument shops). The idea is to strike the fork and gently touch it to one of the silk strands. The spider thinks you are an insect stumbling on his trip wires and will come shooting out to investigate – with bigger species such as *Segestria florentina* they often come out with all guns ablazing and you can actually hear the hard palps strike the metal of the fork – not for the faint of heart! *See panel below.*

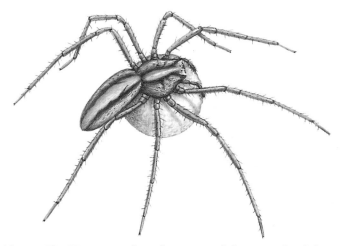

Above: *The Nursery web spider is one of the nomads of the grass jungles of field edge and hedgerow. This female is carrying her egg sac with her, a sight common in mid-summer.*

Certain keys seem to work better than others, although I have had success with C, F and E. The reason for this has nothing to do with the spider's musical preferences but more to do with the sort of vibrations that a struggling insect would produce – but I imagine different-sized insects may struggle at different frequencies which may explain the variation of keys the spiders respond to. If you have trouble getting your hands on a tuning fork, try a party blower with a piece of grass taped to the end. Unravel the tube, hold the grass against one of the threads and blow. Another alternative is simply tickling the web with a blade of grass, although this doesn't always fool the spider.

Experiment: Feel the vibe

1 Strike the tuning fork and touch the 'trip' wires surrounding the spider's lair. Some keys work better than others. I have had success with C, F and E. It has little to do with the spider's musical ear and probably more to do with the frequency of insect wings and legs.

2 By doing this you are fooling the spider into thinking you are an insect. It will rush out from its hideout to attack. *Segestria florentina*, for example, comes out all guns ablazing and you can sometimes hear the fangs hit the fork!

Above: *Crab spider. Why bother building a web, when there are flowers with their own appeal and attraction to passing insects? The Crab spider simply pretends to be a bunch of petals, along comes an innocent insect to pollinate, and stab, stab, suck! This Hedge brown butterfly has uncoiled its proboscis for the last time.*

The second half

This is the back end of the spider; its abdomen. This is less crunchy than the rest of the spiders' body and you can think of it as a kind of living 'water bomb' – a bubble of

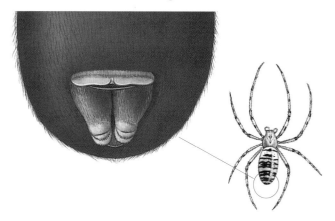

Above: *If you turn your spider upside down in your bug restrainer and look at the end of its abdomen, you should see a device, that can look like little legs or tiny little turrets. These are the spinnerets, the organs that produce and weave the silk that spiders are so famous for.*

spider blood with lots of bits of plumbing, a heart, breathing apparatus, sex organs, guts and the all-important silk glands all contained within a sloshy blood bath.

The size of the abdomen varies. It can be podgy, plump and turgid or withered and shrivelled, big and round or slim and slender, all depending on what species, what sex and at what stage of its life-cycle the spider is.

Super silk
Silk is the spiders' secret of success. It has been described as being as important to spiders as flight is to insects and warm blood is to mammals. Other invertebrates certainly produce silk, caterpillars and caddisfly nymphs to name a couple. But none are more masterly in their use of it than spiders.

Spiders use silk as a building material, safety line, trap, glue and parachute. Silk is a multi-purpose, extra-strong secret weapon of the spider.

'Silknology' – the spider's very talented bottom
Imagine being able to produce from anywhere on your body, yet alone your bottom, a substance with which you could build a house, support many times your body weight, glue things together, catch your food, fly and if at the end of the day all fails you can roll it all up and recycle it! Sounds like the ideal super substance.

Silk is quite remarkable and even though there are other animals that produce it, they are not quite so inventive with it as the spiders. In fact, to a spider silk can almost seem like an extension of its own body, it is a secret weapon, a technology they themselves have mastered.

Silk comes out of the spider's body somewhere around the tip of its bottom. In some species if you look closer you will see tiny little projections that the animal seems to wiggle and wave as it creates – these are called spinnerets. If you were to zoom in with a very powerful microscope you would see on the tip of each spinneret, of which there are six, a forest of lots of little nozzles not unlike those found on cake- icing implements. It is out of these nozzles or spigots that the silk flows.

Silk starts off its life within silk glands in the spider's body. The glands ooze a kind of protein soup that is forced out on the way to the spigots, but contrary to popular belief the silk is not squeezed out of the spider to be hardened by the air. What actually happens is that as the silk gets pulled out of the spigot by the spider, a complicated and rather magical process occurs and the silk stretches and hardens on its own.

This can be observed if you watch a spider descending from the ceiling on a line. Watch what it does with its legs. In the same way someone abseiling, controls the rope as he descends – so does the spider. It has one leg on the line all the time, controlling its rate of descent by pulling the silk out of the spigots.

The silk itself comes in different types for different jobs. The true master craftspiders, the orb web spinners, can produce up to eight different kinds of silk from eight different kinds of silk gland.

Web spinning

1 The spider has to span the gap. It does this by letting the silk drift on the breeze and by jumping or walking between the two points. Once the line is fixed and taut, the spider then crawls along its bridge, spinning a second stretchy loose silk strand. Having attached both ends, the spider then returns to the centre and pulls the second strand down to form the main skeleton.
2 More threads are added, to form the structural spokes of the web, anchoring it well and truly to the surrounding vegetation.
3 The spider then returns to the centre of the web and begins laying down the 'real' trap, the sticky stuff that actually catches the prey. Silk coated with a sticky liquid kind of protein is what makes up the spiral.
4 The web is finally complete, a perfect snare and work of art all in one – we are talking superb form and function here.
5 Depending on the species, the maker of the web will lie in wait, either in the centre of the web or secreted off to one side in a shelter or curled leaf. The spider keeps a foot or two on one of the radial silk spokes, to detect the slightest vibration created by prey getting tangled.

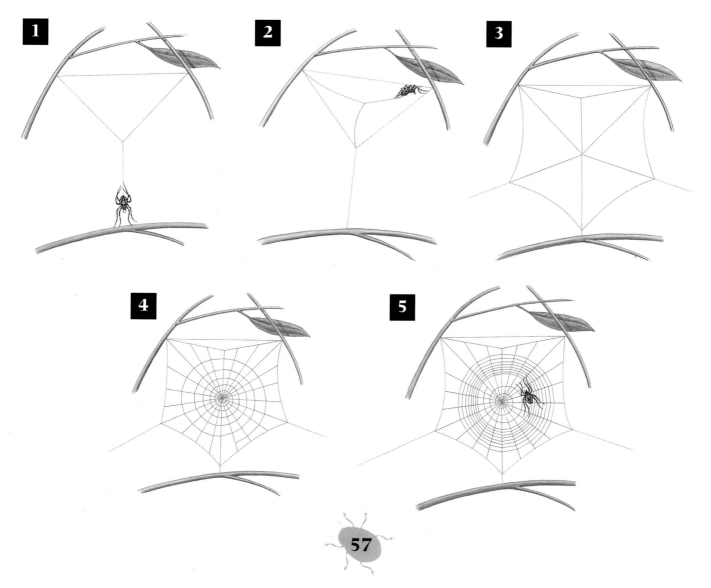

Left: *If this were not showing you a rather beautiful underside, this spider would be instantly recognisable as a common Garden orb spider or Garden cross spider, with a crucifix-like pattern of white spots on its abdomen. Here it is awaiting prey in its web.*

There are nearly as many different designs of web as there are different types of spider, ranging from simple sheets and tangles of silk, the bane of the houseproud to the full-blown masterpiece, the orb web.

If you are too lazy to get up early on an autumn morning to see them at their best, well, you had better get yourself a plant spray – to create your own dew at any time of the day with a fine mist of water, showing webs up to their best effect.

Guild of master craftspiders

If you think of a web, you more than likely dream up an image of the 'classic' orb web – those gorgeous wheel-like structures that decorate many a hedge, gate or fence in the autumn are certainly the most elaborate of all the spiders' craft. It may look pretty to a human eye, but it's true function is more sinister, to snag, catch and snare any insect unfortunate enough to blunder into it.

The orb web – the doily of death

Pretty it may look, wafting in the breeze, covered in baubles of moisture but what you have before you is not a hand woven swatch of Honiton lace but a lethal, efficient, recyclable death trap. It has to be the most advanced of arachnid architecture, made of the minimum of materials, less than 0.5mg of silk is used.

Web spinning

1 This is a very distinctive take on the orb web theme, belonging to two species in the UK, the Wasp spider, Argiope bruennichi *and* Cyclosa conica. *Both spin webs with thick, silk, zigzag stitching worked into the centre. The stitching is known as a* stabilimentum *and nobody can really agree on what it is for.*

2 The webs of spiders that belong to the group Zygiella *are very distinctive. They look like they started well but the spinner did not bother to finish off one corner. However, follow the strand that runs through this 'window' and it will lead you to the home owner, sitting in a retreat, legs on a thread waiting for a bite.*

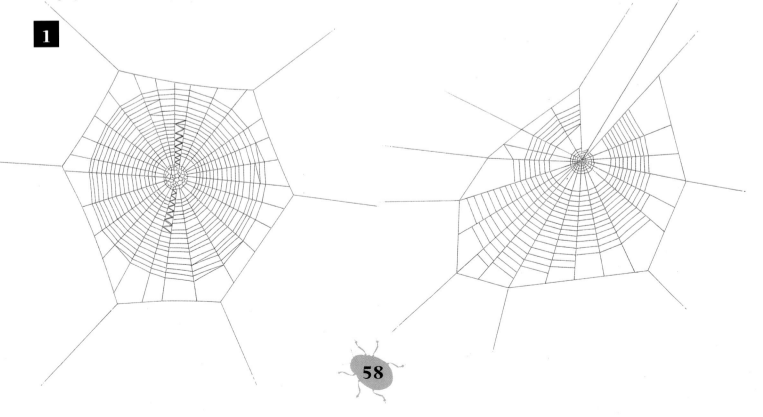

Right: *Just before the egg sac hatches the female Nursery web spider finally lives up to her name, hangs up her boots for the time being, settles down, builds a 'house', the nursery web, and has her family. The egg sac and young are protected in the dense silk construction of the web.*

3 *Many species line their burrows with a silk sock. There are many different designs on this theme. Amourobius spiders can be found making their distinctive funnels in walls, crevices and among the litter. The doormat in this case is the trap. Prey animals get their feet caught up and it is the last trip they make. Look for prey remains.*

4 *This is the design classic, the orb web of the Garden cross spider, the perfect aerial snag, most obvious towards late summer and autumn when these spiders mature.*

3

Making your 'tegenarium'

If you want to learn about everyday spider life there is no better teacher than the House spider. Of all British spiders this is one of the biggest, what's more it's common and lives in and around our homes which makes it easy to find, study and keep. The best way to understand spiders is to keep one as a pet. A simple tank with a few twigs, some damp cotton wool, and a few flies bunged in regularly is all you need to keep one happy. Now you can watch a web being spun.

You will need:
- *plastic aquarium with lid*
- *bark, twigs and soil*
See panel below.

Keep a record of what your spider does, how often it eats and sheds its skin and you will be well on the way to getting to know these amazing little house guests.

Surfing the web

Believe it or not spiders can be found out at sea and in the air, even as high as 3,000 m! They form part of a strange world of aerial plankton that drift around on air currents. They do it by a process known as 'ballooning'. Go out on a dewy autumn morning and you can see why this is. Just about any long grass will be laced with the dew laden

Above: *By gently blowing on the minuscule arachnid, you may get it to demonstrate ballooning for you. It will turn its bottom into the wind and lift its abdomen, issuing forth a silk strand. As soon as the resistance of this silk is enough, the spider will sail off to join the aerial plankton.*

strands of silk, not webs as such but seemingly single strands that link grass blade to grass blade. Investigate closely and you may find the culprits, lots of tiny money spiders, either spiderlings or tiny adults belonging to a family known as *Linyphilids*. If you collect one of these minuscule animals on the tip of your finger and gently blow on it you may persuade it to 'balloon' for you.

If you are lucky, the spider will raise itself up on tip toes and allow the breeze to pull out a thread of silk, which will snake up on the wind. When this develops enough lift to overcome the weight of the micro-spider, it lets go and goes drifting.

Making your 'tegenarium'

1 Put your arachnid in the plastic aquarium. These come complete with a fitting lid, built in ventilation and a hatch, which make feeding your spider easier. Put in a piece of interesting bark, soil and a few twigs. The spider will provide the rest of its abode.
2 As far as food goes, a few flies, or other small creepy-crawlies a week should provide your spider's food and moisture, but there is no harm in dripping a bit of water in, if the place you are keeping your spider is warm. Now watch him spin a web before your eyes.

Experiment: Anyone for tennis?

You will need a coat hanger or bendable wire

Spider silk is the strongest natural material and is weight for weight, length for length stronger than steel. But those strands are so thin it's hard to demonstrate this strength. However, if you collect enough webs you can get some idea of spider silk's remarkable properties.

Take a small loop of stiff wire, bend it around so it has a 'spoon'-like shape (a ring with a handle) and on one of those dewy, cold autumn mornings, try collecting a few webs by placing the wire loop behind the web and drawing it forward. The web should stick. Repeat this several times – try to choose those without residents! Soon you will have lined your 'spoon' with pure spider silk. You can place weights on the collected silk and you will be surprised at how much weight even just a few webs can hold. You can even take a little ball of tin foil and bounce it on the silk you have collected – it shows how strong and stretchy spider silk is. If you have enough silk, you could play a small game of tennis with a friend!

Experiment: Finders keepers

You will need:
- *spray paint*
- *newspaper*
- *artist's fixative or hair spray*
- *coloured card*
- *scissors*

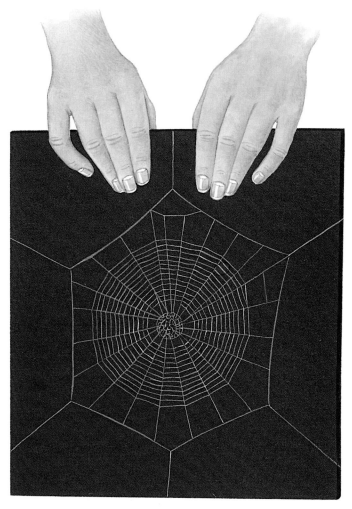

Above: *This trick allows you to preserve a natural work of art. You can measure how much silk is used to make each web and you can frame it and stick it on the wall.*

It sometimes seems a shame to think those gorgeous orb webs that you find draped in the shrubbery or hanging in the hedgerow rarely last longer than a day. Being fragile and ephemeral is of course part of their attraction and from the spider's point of view they are designed as disposable and recyclable insect traps. However, it is possible to preserve these structures and even hang them on your own wall.

First of all, choose a still day and find a real beauty of a web. Make sure it is dry (no droplets of dew) and make sure its maker the spider isn't in residence (check well in and around the edges of the web especially in curled up leaves) as it really won't appreciate what comes next!

Take a can of spray paint – white or black is a good choice – and holding a sheet of newspaper behind the web to stop you getting paint all over the plants or bushes, spray the web evenly and lightly on both sides from a distance of about 40 cm. Too close and you will blow a hole in your web. Leave it to dry for a while and repeat.

The next step is to make your web super sticky. You do this with artist's fixative (available from art and crafts shops). This comes in spray cans like paint and in the same way you coloured your web with paint, spray both sides of the web. You can also use hair spray.

Before it dries, take a bit of card, big enough for your web to fit on and of a colour that contrasts with the colour you sprayed your web. This is the trickiest part of the whole operation; you need to line the card up perfectly with the web and push the card onto the silk so that it sticks in the right place first time. Once the web has touched the card you cannot change your mind without ending up in a messy tangle!

If you've done it right, you should have a perfect web on the card. Use scissors to cut the supporting strands and you can give it another coat of fixative to make sure it's well held in place. You can now mount this spider's original in a frame and hang it on your wall! You could even measure all the strands of silk and work out how much silk was needed to make your web and even collect the orb webs made by different species of spider.

Field guide to common spiders

Garden cross spider

Daddy long legs spider

Daddy long legs spider – Shaking all over

Not to be confused with craneflies or harvestmen all of which have shared the name, this spider is known scientifically as *Pholcus phalangioides*. It is unmistakable, with long gangly hair-like legs and a small unremarkable body. Look under the stairs, in a broom cupboard or in any rarely used corner of your house and you will find this chap sitting in an almost invisible tangle of silk. If you are lucky and find an adult female she could well be with her eggs, which unlike those of many spiders are not shrouded in silk and are clutched like a bunch of grapes. If you are in any doubt about identification gently touch the spider or blow on the web – a daddy long legs will start to vibrate and shake in its web so energetically that it becomes a blur – handy if you want to avoid being eaten.

Garden cross spider – Webmeister

The true master of the web. Of the 40 or so British species that build the pinnacle of silk engineering, the wheel-like orb web, *Araneus diadematus* produces the biggest! The female is one of our heaviest spiders, with an abdomen the size of a pea and even though the colours (which incidentally can be very pretty, with reds, yellows, brown and oranges featuring commonly) are variable, the abdomen always has a distinctive design of a white cross – hence the name. A similar species is the Four-spotted orb spider *Araneus quadratus* that can rival it for size, but is usually darker in colour with four spots arranged on the abdomen replacing the cross.

Woodlouse spider – Devil in the woodpile

Dysdera is a woodlouse specialist, recognisable by its silvery grey abdomen (baked bean size in large specimens) and its rust brown cephalothorax. It prowls around in dark places where its six eyes are not much use.

When it bumps into a woodlouse the spider penetrates its defences with an armour-piercing pair of fangs. The fangs are both long and very mobile and can twist so that one penetrates the woodlouse's belly and the other its back plates. A formidable little spider, it is one of the few that can break human skin, giving an uncomfortable nip to those not careful.

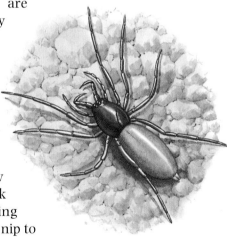

House spider

This species, one of the largest spiders in Europe, frequents undisturbed, dry and dark corners in which our houses abound. Normally they are quite secretive spiders, remaining in their distinctive web, consisting of a triangular sheet with a tubular retreat in one corner. It

62

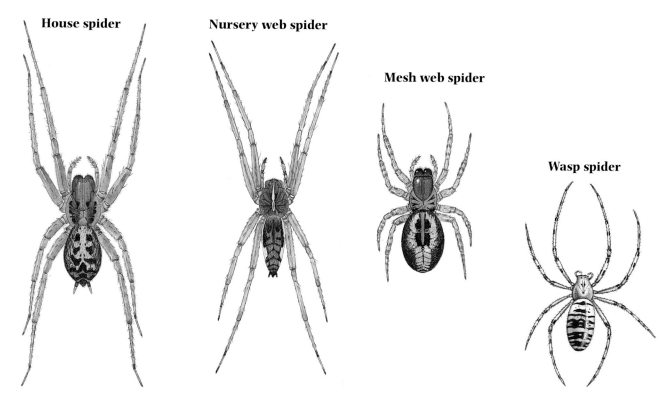

House spider

Nursery web spider

Mesh web spider

Wasp spider

is this species that often find themselves victims of the porcelain pitfalls of our bathroom and kitchen. Contrary to popular belief, they have not emerged from the plug hole. Next time you see one, give it a good close once over and more often than not you will notice the small leg-like limbs nearest the head are tipped with clubs looking a little like miniature boxing gloves – these are the palps (see page 52). These are like sexual pipettes filled with sperm, that are possessed only by the males, and it is these mature males in their wanderings looking for a female that end up being noticed.

Nursery web spider
This is a real beauty. When grown up these spiders are big, with a body length of up to 1.5 cm and an impressive leg span. They always look slick and smooth, the colour of peanut butter, with a pale beige stripe down the centre of their backs and white 'go-faster' stripes down the length of their sides. Being webless spiders for most of the year, they hunt among the long grass and brambles of the countryside and they are often to be seen resting with their legs stretched out on plant stems in a characteristic position with the front two pairs of legs held together. These are gorgeous spiders to keep and watch for a while and if you are lucky enough to catch an adult male and female you may witness a bit of spider 'chivalry'. A true gentlemen to the end, the male offers the female an insect meal wrapped up in silk before he mates with her. This isn't simply a generous

act, it is a matter of survival – if she didn't have the meal to eat then she would make a meal of him instead!

Mesh web spider
These small spiders live in holes in walls and fences. They line their holes with a silk sock and then surround their front door with a mesh of messy thin silk, looking a bit like a small hairnet. This is made of silk strands with a tangle of loops of stretchy silk loosely wrapped around it (a type known as cribellate silk). This trap works like the hoops on velcro, an insect's feet and hairs being the hooks. The spider waits in its lair for an insect to stumble into its net, before pouncing.

Wasp spider – The funky one!
The female of the wasp spider, *Argiope bruennichi*, is a fat-bottomed beauty, with enough black, yellow and white stripes to make a tiger jealous.

A member of the orb web spinning spiders, the female sits plum in the middle of her web, fairly low to the ground in grassy and scrubby vegetation. Most of the webs spun by the female are also unusual among British spiders in having stabilimentum – thick, wavy silk spokes that radiate from the hub. It has never been common. First discovered in the UK in Sussex in the 1940s, it has since then been playing bust and boom all over the shop, with colonies now spotted all along the south coast centred around the Hampshire and Dorset coastline.

Crab spider

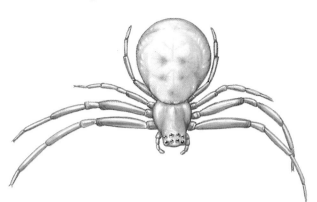

Zebra spider

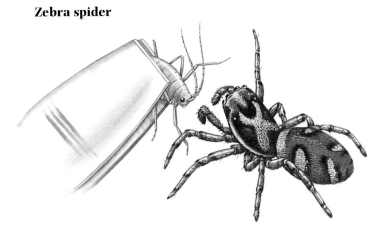

Crab spider – The beautiful assassin

Another spider that does without silk to make its living. Female crab spiders can get quite chunky and have a very distinctive shape, a wide flattened body with long first two pairs of legs and as their name suggests they move with an ungainly crab-like sideways gait. There are several species that you may come across in the exploration of your garden. All are masters of camouflage. A particularly pretty and common species is *Misumena vatia*. She can be a real babe of a spider and comes in both a yellow form and a white form – easy to see you might think. Well, in theory yes, but when I tell you they hang out in yellow and white flowers respectively, things get a little trickier.

The best way to find these spiders is to look in every yellow and white flower you come across during the early summer and eventually you will find one. They are a spider that has mastered the act of ambush – look like the flower you are sitting on and as long as you are quick you can grab any insect that pops in for pollen and nectar. The design of the spider helps her, those long

Below: The Water spider spins a sheet-like web underwater, storing bubbles of air beneath it to create a diving bell.

front legs are spiny and embrace the prey, often a much larger bee or butterfly in a lethal hug, biting quickly behind the head to stop it struggling, all the time holding onto the flower with her hind pair of legs.

Feed the zebra

The tiny hyperactive Zebra spider, *Salticus scenicus*, resides on hot sunny walls and is often seen on window-sills in spring and summer. These spiders make up for their size by sheer personality. If ever there was a spider that deserved the title of being cute then this one is it! Part of what makes this animal so appealing are its eyes – it has the standard set of eight but these are dominated by a pair of particularly large beady ones that take up most of the front of the spiders' 'face'. It is therefore not much of a surprise to learn that these animals have some of the best eyesight of any British spider, apparently able to detect movement 30 cm away.

Water spiders – Extraordinary aquanauts

Probably one of the most adventurous ways of life for a spider is that adopted by the water spider, *Argyroneta aquatica*. Not only were these spiders using scuba technology before humans, they also invented the diving bell. The only way of tracking them down is by pond-dipping in weedy waterways with a net. As an animal it looks quite dull – but pop it in a small tank with water weed and it starts to create its own little Atlantis. Water spiders can breathe under the surface by trapping a layer of air around their abdomen. This appears as a silver bubble which they can crawl around with – they have special hairs for this. Being related to the house spiders, they also spin a sheet-like web, under water. They then make trips to the surface, collecting bubbles of air which they rub off under the sheet – this becomes buoyant and stretches, eventually forming a dome. Here is the clever bit: once built, the sheets rarely have to be restocked with air because as oxygen is used up, fresh oxygen gets absorbed into the diving bell.

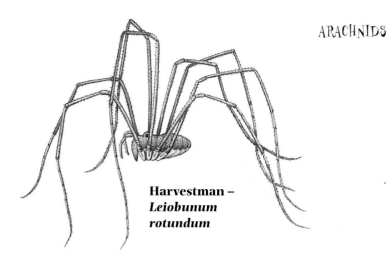

**Harvestman –
*Leiobunum
rotundum***

**Harvestman –
*Nemastoma bimaculatum***

Above: *With long lever-like legs and a button-like body, it's easy to see why this common species,* Leiobunum rotundum, *has many other groovy names, like air crab.*

Above: *Daddy short legs! Not all harvestmen are blessed in the limb department. This one,* Nemastoma bimaculatum, *is found among the leaf litter.*

Harvestman – The spider that isn't

Lift ivy that has grown against walls, look amongst ferns and thick vegetation, in dark corners of the shed and under windowsills and you are sure to turn up a gangly life form that when disturbed wobbles off in a manic random sprint that is seemingly better co-ordinated than its cotton fine legs should allow! The Brazilian name for them, which I rather like, is *giro mundo*, which refers to their speed and agility. We know them as harvestmen, owing to their apparent appearance towards the end of summer onwards. This is when they mature and are largest and hence more evident.

The technical name for harvestmen as a family are the *Opiliones*. We have something like 23 species in Britain but even after a leg count has revealed eight legs,

it is a surprise to some to find that they are not spiders at all, although in the same order that contains spiders, scorpions and ticks, the Arachnids.

They differ from spiders, which they superficially resemble, by not having any poison glands, not being able to produce silk and by having their body parts fused together to form a single button-like body, suspended usually when active between the long vegetation-spanning legs. If you have any doubts about identification, look at the body: a harvestman is an all-in-one affair, no two halves here!

Harvestmen are curious creatures that hang around in shady places where it is moist, under window-sills, behind ivy or up against the shed eaves – only emerging to feed by night.

Red spider mite– The biggest of the mites and one I come across regularly sunning itself on a spring morning on the walls of my garden is the Red spider mite, which looks like a small bobble off your granny's favourite curtains that has come to life.

Sheep tick
You are most likely to encounter this parasite in the ears and around the head of your dog after it has been in long undergrowth. These creatures have complicated lifecycles and rely on the chance that a suitable host will pick them up, where they feed on blood. Deer and sheep are the usual hosts.

Pseudoscorpion
Over 25 species of these little creatures – the biggest is only about 5 mm long – live in the UK. Completely harmless to us, they have no sting in their tail, but they do have pincers loaded with poison glands, to tackle their minute prey deep in the leaf litter and compost. Look for them by spreading out leaf litter on a white sheet and investigating with a magnifying lens.

Introducing the Insects

Insects are the most successful life form on the planet. There are more than one million different species and scientists estimate there could be anything from three to ten million! This makes them also one of the least explored animal groups; we know so little about them and it is this that makes even the most basic backyard science exciting. Insects include, butterflies, moths, dragonflies, damselflies, crickets, grasshoppers, wasps, bees, ants, bugs, beetles and flies.

Body design

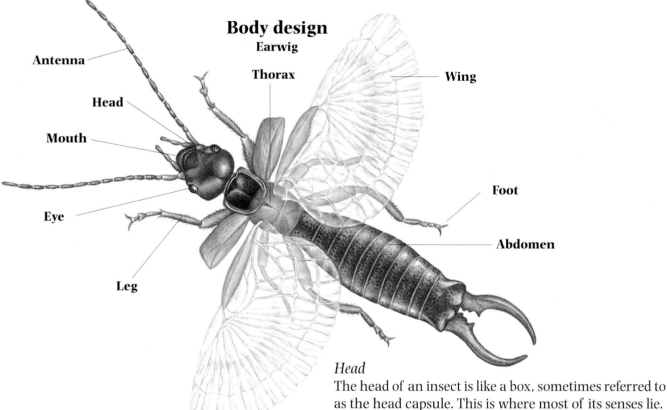

Antenna

Head

Mouth

Eye

Leg

Earwig

Thorax

Wing

Foot

Abdomen

Head
The head of an insect is like a box, sometimes referred to as the head capsule. This is where most of its senses lie.

If you find yourself spending more and more time with your head in a specimen pot, looking through a magnifying lens and shouting 'Ooooh, what on earth is that!', the chances are your friends and family are worried you may sprout wings and antennae soon. Congratulations! You have just become an Entomologist!

What makes an insect an insect?
Despite a confusing array of shapes and sizes, insects all have a basic body plan. All insects have six legs and three main body sections: a head, thorax and abdomen. Of all the invertebrates only insects have wings, but not *all* insects have wings! If it's a creepy-crawly and it's capable of flight, it is beyond doubt an insect.

Antennae
Sometimes these are called feelers, but they do a lot more than simply feel and touch; on these often moving bits are organs sensitive to smell, taste and vibration.

Eyes
Some insects can detect light through their skin or cuticle but most have specialised eyes, ranging from very simple single eyes, called *ocelli*, that probably do no more than detect whether it is light or dark, to very complicated, compound eyes, like a dragonfly's. Compound eyes can have thousands of lenses and are very sensitive to movement and probably have a pretty good view on the detail in the world too. Some insects have very good colour vision and can even see ultra-violet.

Mouth

Not all insects have a working mouth. Some moths don't bother feeding – all their time is taken up by breeding! But those that do feed have a variety of mouth shapes and structures. Some are a bit like our jaws but work from side to side rather than up and down. They can be designed for biting and shearing through plants; others are used as meat slicers. Some are flattened to crush seeds. They can also manipulate stuff like mud and paper and so have been modified into spades and trowels. Some get stretched to crazy proportions and are used as weapons against prey, predators and each other.

Thorax

This is the engine room of the insect. Look for the bit of the body with all the legs and wings sticking out of it! Inside this are the muscles that drive the legs and wings.

Legs

Six legs provide stability and efficiency; the insect moves in such a way that there is always three legs on the ground, like a tripod. Many insects have modified their legs for jumping, swimming, digging and battling. Legs can detect the state of the world – many insect's legs have sensory hairs that feel, taste, smell and hear.

Feet

Insect feet are very sensitive to what they are treading on – they have lots of spikes, bristles and hooks. They keep the insect's antennae, eyes and body clean. Other feet are like grappling hooks used to grip onto things. At the tip of their feet some insects have a special pad covered in thousands of tiny hairs with flattened tips, these stick to surfaces, and by oozing grease they work in the same way a wet drinks coaster sticks to a glass.

Wings

Not every insect has wings but when they are present there are two pairs. Some forewings are modified as protective coverings for the rear ones. Other wings are joined by little hooks so that although there are four wings they act as two. Some insects use their wings for display and the production of sound like crickets.

Abdomen

All the organs to do with digestion, storage of food, the heart are found in this part of the insect's body.

Spiracles

Lots of little tubes, called trachea, act like the ventilation ducts in an office building. The air gets in via a system of tiny holes called spiracles, found down the side of its body.

Above: *Insects come in a wide variety of shapes, but follow the same basic pattern. Wasps belong to the order* Hymenoptera, *along with bees, ants and sawflies.*

Above: *This Pond skater or Water strider is a very common aquatic bug. It skims the surface of ponds and lakes but its feet never get wet.*

Above: *Beetles are the largest order of insects, Coleoptera. There are more than 350,000 different beetle species known to science.*

Butterflies and Moths – Flights of Fancy

Think of butterflies and moths and we have the perfect public relations agents for the insect world. The popular image of butterflies as harmless, flouncy, care-free insects flitting idly from flower to flower is, I admit, an attractive one, accentuated by the fact that they mainly fly on the sort of days we like, namely, calm sunny ones!

The fascination for moths resides in their mastery of camouflage and the mystique of the night. These delicate animals are subject to the same pressures of living, feeding and breeding as the more ugly insects and other invertebrates that star in this book. They fight their own battles, armed to the proboscis with weapons, nasty chemicals or itchy hairs. They deceive, murder and bribe their way through their lives.

Butterfly or moth?

When someone hands me a caterpillar, or points out a flying adult and asks me whether it's a moth or a butterfly, I can usually tell them. When they ask me 'Why?', I start having a bit of trouble. In the same way a birdwatcher can identify a bird by what they call its 'jizz' (a combination of look, movement and shape), I deal with butterflies and moths in the same way.

So what makes a butterfly a butterfly, or a moth a moth? Well, they are pretty much the same thing, but here is a basic comparison.

Above: *Butterflies and moths are the insects that most people identify with. This one got very friendly!*

The scientific name for the order of butterflies and moths is *Lepidoptera* (*Lepis* for scale and *Pteron* for wing).

Wing position
Butterflies rest with their wings closed above their body and moths rest with theirs horizontally.

Colours and patterns
Butterflies are supposed to be colourful, moths dull and dreary, everybody knows that. Now find a picture of a Dingy skipper (a butterfly) or go and look at the pinks and greens of an Elephant hawk moth, and tell me that still holds true. Generally speaking you need to look a bit closer for the beauty of moths, while butterflies are much more in your face.

Antennae
The technical names of butterflies and moths, *Rhopalocera* for butterflies and *Heterocera* for moths, describe their antennae. For butterflies it means 'clubbed antennae' and for moths it means 'different antennae'.

Scales on wings
Both butterflies and moths have wings covered in tiny scales. These give them their patterns and coloration.

Body size
Both butterflies and moths have bodies with some covering of hair-like scales, these tend to be a little longer

Body design

Antennae

Wings

Above: *A Painted lady butterfly showing classic butterfly traits – bright colours, thin body and clubbed antennae. Butterflies rest with their wings closed and upright.*

Above: *A Herald moth. Big chunky body, more dowdy with string-like antennae. This comparison is easy but it gets a little fluffier to tell moth from butterfly with other species.*

and more pronounced in night-flying moths. These hairs can make the body look bigger. But some moths do have thin bodies, especially the smaller geometrids and the grass moths.

Moths fly by night, butterflies by day, yet another rule that is on the whole correct. There are a few day-flying moths. In the tropics there are also a few night-flying butterflies.

A word on nets

I'm not going to endorse the use of butterfly nets here. It is all too easy to turn someone into a net-wielding maniac that just gets hung up on the thrill of the chase and the final capture, a mentality I would prefer to leave with the Victorian collectors. I still stick to my belief that eyeballs are best for learning about butter-flies and moths.

But nets do have their uses, particularly when you are just beginning and are having trouble identifying that little brown butterfly that keeps whizzing around and then shooting off like a miniature jet fighter, before you can say the word 'Fritillary' and get your field guide.

If this is you, then with the correct use of a butterfly net and the right kind of observation pots, you can catch, bag and identify your beast without even laying a finger on it.

Use the net gently, picking the insects from vegetation or from behind in flight. Try to avoid swiping with the net as this can damage the fragile wings. If the insect is flying, swing the net from behind and, with a quick flick of the wrist, fold the net, trapping the butterfly or moth in the bag.

Once you have your insect in the net, you can lift up the end of the net bag and allow the insect to fly or crawl up toward the light.

Pill boxes
The next step is to identify it. Nets, even black ones that allow better views of your subject, may not give you a clear enough view of the details you need to see.

I tend to transfer the insect gently to a special card-board pot with a clear bottom. These can be bought for a matter of pennies from special entomological suppliers and go under the name of pill boxes.

Alternatively, you can make your own pill boxes. Cut up some toilet rolls and tape a cardboard lid to one end. Then make a removable lid out of some clear plastic for the other end. Tape the lid into position so that your specimens don't escape.

Butterflies and moths can be transferred to a pill box by gently cupping it over the insect as it rests in the net and sliding the lid on. The advantage of the clear bottom is that the insects will crawl toward the light, making it easy to manoeuvre and not unwittingly trap wings and legs.

The butterfly or moth can now be identified at leisure. Use a small torch to shed extra light on them if you need to pick out tiny details.

Left: *Having said I'm not going to endorse nets too much, they do have their uses and here is a picture of me trying to catch a small butterfly for close identification.*

A real Easter egg hunt

The best way to find eggs is to watch the adult insects. This is obviously easier with butterflies. It helps if you know the food plants of the insects you are watching. Common species such as Small tortoiseshell and Peacock make egg laying rather obvious. They choose stinging nettles as their food plant and one of the best times to watch out for them is in the spring when the adults have been out of hibernation for a couple of weeks and are desperate to get down to the business of breeding. Look in sunny corners of fields and wasteland where the nettles are just beginning to grow and look fresh and succulent. Female butterflies, when they are searching for a place to lay their eggs, shop around, keeping low, touching down briefly to taste the leaves with their feet.

When they find the perfect nibble for their caterpillars, they curl their abdomen under the leaf and often keep fluttering their wings. This is now time to concentrate; get too close and you will disturb her. Hold back and as soon as she flies away memorise her position and go and look. Gently turning over the leaves on the plant she was on should reveal a cluster of glassy green eggs. Some butterflies never settle to lay eggs; some scatter their eggs like salt while flying over clumps of their caterpillar food plant, so it helps to know basic background information on the species you are studying.

Metamorphosis or magic?

Butterflies and moths rebuild themselves several times, a transformation that is so extreme that they look and behave like very different animals.

Egg – The world's smallest box of tricks

Butterfly and moth eggs are amazing. Wacky colours and markings abound and some come in such bizarre shapes they look like spiky golf balls or super ornate crystal green houses.

Some eggs are laid singly, others in clumps and clusters, some are sprinkled far and wide and some are plastered with hairs. It is impossible to generalise and show you how to find all of them, but there are a few general rules and techniques (see *A real Easter egg hunt*).

The caterpillar hunter

Caterpillars come in as many fascinating shapes, sizes and colours as the adult insects themselves. Their job is to eat and grow as quickly as possible while all the time avoid being eaten themselves.

The problem is nearly every animal that eats insects is also looking for caterpillars, so many have developed neat tricks to help them play the ultimate game of hide and seek.

Night time is the right time

Many caterpillars feed only at night when predators are out of the way. The best way of finding these chaps is to invest in a good focusable torch and a set of rechargeable batteries. It helps to do a bit of detective work first, though. When out and about by day look for chomping signs – big chunks and crescent shapes taken out of the edges of leaves are a good clue. In cities the presence of real monsters like the caterpillars of Lime, Privet and Poplar hawk moths is often given away by the distinctive round droppings scattered on the pavements under suitable food trees or overhanging hedges.

The problem with looking for these jelly monsters of the moth world by day is that they have a neat camouflage, with patterns that break up their outline and colours that blend into their surroundings. But at night they relax and move around, often heading for more succulent leaves at the ends of twigs and branches.

Using a torch, you can pick them out rather easily, just by shape alone. One of the advantages of 'caterpillaring' by the power of a torch, is that not only does a bit

Above: Every year I get phone calls in the summer from distraught people having found a snake in among their fuchsias! It is usually not so at all but the large and spectacular caterpillar of the Elephant hawk moth.

of artificial light blow their cover for some reason, by disrupting their usual camouflage, but the fact your light is often coming from below or from the side and not from above as nature intended means that all those disruptive patterns do not work.

Don't beat around the bush, beat the bush!

One of the best ways of finding lots of different caterpillars and many other groovy insects for that matter is a technique used by many professional bug hunters, known as 'beating'. The idea is that you knock the insects out of the bushes or trees in which they live. You need something to beat the bush with – a stout stick or broom handle – lots of collecting pots (you'll be surprised at how many interesting bugs will fall your way) and something to collect the caterpillars on when they fall.

You can buy purpose-made beating trays, but an upturned umbrella or an old white bed sheet will do just as well. The technique is simple; hold your umbrella under the bush or branch of your choice, or spread out your sheet, then take your stick and strike or shake the foliage. There is a knack to this; if you are too gentle, you will simply make any insects grip on even tighter and they will be hard or impossible to dislodge by further shaking and beating. So make the first strike count! The idea is to catch them off guard and they will lose their grip and fall your way.

Right: Spread a white sheet, umbrella, card, or a beating tray under a bush and give the bush a hearty thwack with a stick – you will be surprised what falls out!

Above: *Pink elephants flying! The Elephant hawk moth's bright colours act as a deterrent to predators that get too close. They are startling to say the least, showing that moths are not always dull, grey and brown.*

Below: *The baby Eyed hawk moth survives by not looking like the big, juicy, caterpillar it is. All those greens and the oblique lines down its side break up its outline.*

The night is also a handy time to locate the secretive and rarely seen caterpillars of the very common brown butterflies, such as Meadow brown and Gatekeeper. You will need to work low down in long grass. Get down on the level of the tender grass shoots themselves and with a bit of luck you will pick out the shapes of small brown and green caterpillars.

Walking stomachs

Put simply, caterpillars are stomachs with legs; they eat for a living. Born into a salad bowl, they are completely surrounded by food and their job is simple. They are the part of the lifecycle that gathers all the raw materials that will be of use to it in later life as a flying adult butterfly or moth.

Just look at their heads. Use a hand lens and choose as large a caterpillar as possible. The head itself speaks volumes about what matters to the caterpillar. The head capsule, together with the segments of the legs, are the only bits of the body that contain chitin, the hard stuff, that makes the exoskeleton of most other invertebrates.

On the head you may find a cluster of simple eyes (these are of use to recognise light and dark only) and near them, either side of the mouth, a pair of tiny downward pointing antennae to taste and feel the food. The

Garden tiger **Pale tussock** **Peacock**

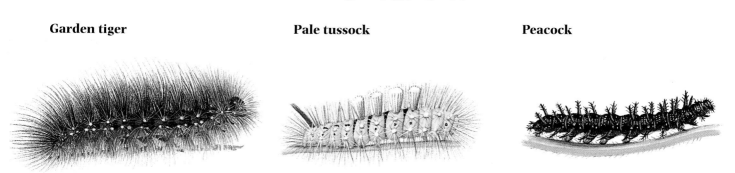

mouth, however, is a marvel of scissor-like plates that mash, mangle and masticate plant matter full time.

Other notable features include the spiracles, tiny holes for breathing that all insects have spaced out down the side of their bodies. They can be tricky to see in other insects, but in smooth, non-hairy caterpillars they stand out a treat.

Count the legs. A golden rule of insects is that they have six legs, but caterpillars have decided somewhere in their evolution that six legs were not enough for their lifestyle, so they cheated and developed a few more! They still have six true legs, made of hard material and with joints, clustered near the head. The other eight legs found toward the back end of the caterpillar are extras called pro-legs. They are soft and end in a collection of Velcro-like hooks.

The rest of the caterpillar's body is really a soft, flexible and expandable sac, a good example of a moveable and soft exoskeleton.

Earlier on I mentioned the tough skeleton supporting an insect's body. This is an exception; the support for caterpillars comes from the body fluid inside, which is kept at pressure. The simple skin means it is easy to get out of, meaning caterpillars can grow very quickly, shedding their skins once or even twice a week.

Growing quickly is handy, but the price caterpillars must pay for this convenience is they do not have the armoured protection of other insects.

Forts, fuzz, bristles and spines

Soft, saggy bags of guts they may be but caterpillars have an armoury of tricks and gadgets that are spectacularly good at allowing them to make it to life with wings.

Just look at one of those caterpillars you have probably come across when beating bushes. The only reason you can spot them is because you have knocked them out of their world and onto your sheet – put one back on a twiggy branch and it vanishes instantly. These animals do perfect stick impressions, as others do a good version of leaves, bark and even, in the case of the Comma butterfly, a bird's dropping!

Above: *Just a selection of the weird and wonderful world that is the caterpillar. I challenge anyone to not be a little scared of those bristles.*

Defence

Another use of colour is as a warning. Some caterpillars steal nasty chemicals from the plants on which they feed, giving them an unpleasant taste. These caterpillars, such as the piebald caterpillar of the Magpie moth and the rugby jersey striped Cinnabar moth caterpillar, advertise themselves by being brightly coloured.

Other animals learn from experience that these leave an unpleasant taste in the mouth and so leave them alone. Some caterpillars use this warning because they carry poisonous itchy hairs (this particular caterpillar defence works all too well on humans too and will leave you with a painful rash, or very sore and swollen eyes if you rub them after touching one of these caterpillars).

Next time you see a group of Peacock or Small tortoiseshell caterpillars feeding, touch the leaf they are on and watch what happens. These guys have many levels of defence. During their early days they feed as a group, which gives them safety in numbers. They also have a body covered in spines. If you disturb them they will all twitch their heads together, giving the impression of an animal bigger than a mere caterpillar. If this doesn't work they will vomit gobs of green liquid and hold it towards their attacker; this may taste bad or simply make them a less pleasant meal. If all of these tactics fail, the caterpillars simple roll off the leaf and fall down to the base of the nettles on which they feed, where they are extremely tricky to find.

Pupa and chrysalis

Pupa means 'doll or puppet' and can be used for both moths and butterflies. Chrysalis means 'golden', referring to the metallic sheen on some, and is used exclusively for butterflies.

Act Three ... and now for something completely different!

Assuming our caterpillar makes it this far, there will come a day when it prepares to moult again. There may be a few clues that this is not to be like any of the other skin changes so far made in its life. Some change colour and their brightness disappears. Certain moths will bury themselves in soil, others will weave a silken sleeping bag around their bodies. Butterflies, like Small tortoiseshells, may hang upside down, curling their head up in a J shape. Some, like Cabbage whites, remain head up, but spin a little waist harness around their middle. Then for the last time incarnated as a caterpillar, the head capsule pops off, the skin splits and is shrugged off, revealing a 'thing'. I say a thing because at this stage it looks like nothing alive.

It has no features to speak of, no limbs, or eyes, although if you look close enough you can make out in some species the strange mask-like impressions of legs, eyes antennae and wings of the animal to be. But if it wasn't for the odd twitch and wriggle, there is nothing that would give you a clue that this is a life form.

This is stage three in the lifecycle of a butterfly or moth. What has just been created is the pupa or chrysalis.

This skin is the casket that holds one of the most mind-blowing transformations in the world. Within, the caterpillar becomes an adult butterfly or moth, but it doesn't change gradually. It dissolves into a rather disgusting living soup, a gunk of cells, and rebuilds itself as another animal altogether.

Although this is an event worthy of a fanfare, the reality is that it all occurs very quietly – a chrysalis or pupa is still a tasty snack for many animals and so they rely on the same defences as they did as a caterpillar. Some have amazing sculptural qualities about them, particularly the exposed chrysalids of most butterflies, bedecked with weird appendages, lumps, bumps and flanges designed to break up their outline.

Others are camouflaged and some play with light – a trick that is done entirely with mirrors. The chrysalis of

Comma lifecycle

1 The eggs of the Comma butterfly, soon to hatch.
2 The caterpillar feeds on nettles, constantly eating to fatten itself up to prepare itself for its metamorphosis into a butterfly.
3 Now the caterpillar has cryptically camouflaged itself to match its surroundings; it looks like a dead leaf, but is in fact the pupa or chrysalis. This disguise is in order to deter preditators.
4 Once the pupa emerges as an adult butterfly or imago it will soon start taking nectar from flowers.

Tortoiseshell lifecycle

The silken web provides a modicum of protection from larger predators but not the insidious attention of a parasitic wasp.

Freshly hatched larvae gather in clots beneath the web where they feed furiously on the succulent leaf tips.

Pregnant females search the nettle bed for areas free of caterpillars that could compete with her potential brood.

Female Tortoiseshell egg laying onto a soft fresh and succulent shoot, an ideal meal for her brood.

More mature larvae forage singly, having left the security of the web and rely on wriggling and dropping from the leaf to escape larger predators.

The cryptic chrysalis hangs in the shade for 2-3 weeks before the adult emerges.

many *Nymphalid* butterflies, which include the Peacock and Small tortoiseshell, have metallic panels that reflect their background and bounce light around. Others disguise themselves as leaves.

Moths go underground or surround themselves with a fortress, a cocoon of silk, produced by glands in the caterpillar's mouth.

Experiment: Digging in the dirt

There is nothing more perfect than the pupa of a moth. All conker shiny, red, brown or orange, many sit out the winter months in this stage of their life cycle between caterpillar and adult moth. To find these take an old margarine tub of soil or moss, a trowel and a hand fork, and gently dig around the bases of trees. Do not tear up the soil or go any deeper than 10 cm.

Be patient and you will find the gems you are after. In my experience certain trees are better than others. The best are the willows, sallows and poplar.

Sterilise some soil or moss (10 minutes in a microwave oven), place it in a seed tray or tub and arrange your pupae collection on this. Keep it in a cool place such as a shed or garage out of the sun and spray with water once a week, making sure that the soil is always damp but not soggy. Place a few sticks in the soil so the moths have something to climb up.

If you have found your pupae in the autumn or winter, they will probably not hatch until the following spring, but any other time of the year and you will just have to keep checking, they could hatch at any time.

Flamboyant finale – adult butterfly or moth

Then comes the day that the pupa splits, revealing a creature nothing like the caterpillar. It has a weird head, consisting entirely of eyes – big ones too, not the simple specks of the caterpillar but large, googly, multi-faceted affairs. There are long antennae and in most species, not a mouth with two obvious jaws, but two half tubes which are zippered up early on after emergence and are used like a straw, to drink fluid such as nectar, fermenting fruit, sap, water or urine. This mouth is coiled up like a hose pipe and held under the head.

If you raise caterpillars and actually get to watch this event, just take a moment to reflect on the naked butterfly or moth. Without wings, which on emergence are all scrunched up, they really are quite ugly. But just wait a while longer.

To start with this creature is trapped between two worlds. With six spindly legs not best designed for walking, it drags itself up to a position where it can hang freely. It now pumps blood into the veins in the wings, allowing them to expand. The liquid hardens and sets, leaving a pair of stiff wings ready for the air.

Wings – not just for flying!

A butterfly's wings are not just a beautiful array of colours and patterns, they are survival devices and fulfil jobs beyond propelling the insect through the air.

Radiators
Wings are used like radiators. Butterflies need to get their body temperature up to around 30°C to be active. Held open, wings can be used as solar panels, to warm the blood in them and take it back to the insect's body. This is the familiar basking pose adopted by many butterflies when the air temperature is cool, during the early morning hours.

Above: *The bright forewings of this butterfly are like shiny copper, hence its name Small copper. Its caterpillars are small and green. It flies during summer months.*

Flags
The bright funky patterns of the day-flying butterflies and moths are like flags. They act as signals to others of the same species. Like colours in a football team, these distinctive patterns and hues allow them to communicate with one another, particularly useful when trying to find a mate. The colours and patterns of moths are chiefly to help them hide during the daylight hours.

Bright wing colours also act as a warning. In most species the gaudy is combined with sombre colours that can hide these flash markings.

The Peacock butterfly is a good example of this. Imagine being a bird and stumbling across a few of these butterflies hibernating. The subtle patterns on the undersides of their wings this time have not worked, you are about to take a bite when suddenly 'ssshisssh!', four purple eyes are staring right back at you. These combined with the noise (yet another surprising use for wings created by rubbing the fore- and hindwings together) are enough to scare off the bird.

Attack deflectors

The other use of eye-spots and in fact spots in general is to deflect an attack. If you study a population of Meadow browns or Gatekeepers you will notice that a lot of them have bits of their wings missing. Sometimes these triangular chunks taken out of the wing have been caused by birds trying to catch them. The bird has aimed at the targets on the wings, and the wing has just broken away allowing the butterfly to fly another day.

This is taken to the extreme in the Blue and Hairstreak butterflies. The undersides of their wings also have an eyespot at the corner of the rearwing, and some species have another blotch of colour and a tail, which looks just like a second head with antennae. The bird or predator makes a similar mistake and lunges for the dummy head instead of the real one – the butterfly could end up losing a bit of its wing, but at least it has not lost its head! A life-saving disguise.

Sooner or later you will be rummaging in the garden shed, when a huge brightly coloured orange moth zooms past your ear. That was an Orange underwing. If you now went looking for the moth you would be searching for a bright orange insect; the moth has tricked you, just like it would trick a predator. The moth is not allowing you to see it as it is hiding the orange wings under a camouflaged cloak of the brown and grey dappled forewings.

Perfume wafters

A surprising use of wings is as wafters of sexy perfume. Many male butterflies have very special scales on the surface of the wings, called scent scales, designed to break off, complete with a perfume that has oozed onto them from glands on the wings. These scent scales are used in courtship. Some butterflies draw the female's smelling organs, her antennae, over the scales. Other male butterflies simply vibrate their wings in such a way as to show the female.

Just look at the wings of male Gatekeepers. One of the distinguishing features is a dark smudge in the middle of the orange bit of the forewing. This is a patch of those special scales.

Make a butterfly decoy

Place a scrap of white rag about the size of a butterfly on the end of a piece of wire (try a straightened out coat

Above: *The Small emerald moth flies at night from June to August. They can commonly be seen on downland, in hedges or at woodland edges.*

hanger). Now do a jerky, wobbly butterfly impression with it in an area where other white butterflies are flying. You will find that curious males will come to investigate your decoy, then on realisation that it isn't genuine, they will fly on. You can cut butterfly shapes out of cardboard to demonstrate the same thing, different colours will interest other species.

Experiment: All sweetness ...

Most butterflies and moths fuel all their flapping about and chasing around with an energy-rich, sugary diet. This can be nectar from flowers and some species have a love for fermenting fruit like rotting apples and oozing sap. This is particularly useful to those of us who want to study moths.

Moths are notorious boozers, so a great way to see some species is to provide the drinks. Lepidopterists have used this technique known as 'sugaring' to attract moths for hundreds of years.

The principle is to make a cocktail, and it doesn't matter all that much what you put in it as long as it has the qualities of stickiness, sweetness and it is smelly enough to tickle the antennae of moths some distance away and to attract them to come and try the cocktail.

Making your sugaring for moths

1 Mix together all the ingredients.
2 Gently heat and stir adding water or sugar to get the consistency quite runny. When you have made your mix you will fill the house with a sickly smell and probably commandeer the kitchen for an afternoon.
3 All you need to do now is to wait until dusk, preferably on a warm summer's night, and taking a jam jar full of the sugaring solution and a stout paint brush apply the mix generously to tree trunks and fence posts in your garden. If you vary the positions and habitats, you are more likely to see more kinds of moth.
4 Return to your posts an hour or so later with a torch and see what you have lured out of the night.
5 An alternative is to make a runnier mixture and soak old rags in it, these can then be hung up around the place to the same effect.

Recipes for the best 'sugaring' mix are a very personal thing; you can tweak and taste, mix and improve. Entomologists of old have closely guarded their own secret brew, but here is a basic one, which I have used to great success, to start you off.

You will need:
- *big pan*
- *paint brush*
- *sugar*
- *molasses*
- *fruit juice*
- *dark rum*

- *torch*
- *jam jar*
- *water*
- *rags*

See panel above.

Experiment: ... and light!

The other well known, but less easy to explain, attraction for moths is light. It has been observed for years that moths are attracted to the flame, or its 20th century equivalent, the light bulb. But nobody really knows why they do it. Probably the most believable of ideas is that somehow nocturnal insects including moths use distant sources of light such as the moon for navigation when flying at night.

The idea is that the moth keeps the moon lighting up the same part of its eye. Try it for yourself. On a moonlit night walk with the moon in the same place say to your

right or left, keep it there in the same part of your field of vision and you will move in a straight line. But when man started lighting up the night with his own lamps, candles and bulbs, the moths got confused.

Get a friend to stand in one spot with a torch. Try the same thing as before, and you will find that to keep the light from the torch shining in the same place in your field of vision you will need to turn your body as you walk. Eventually you will end up bumping into your mate! This is because the torch is much closer to you than the moon.

This situation is exploited by mothy people; to find out what moths are around they use a special light, a mercury vapour, or black light, positioned over a trap with a collection bucket and a funnel of some kind. You can buy traps from entomological suppliers but they tend to be expensive.

When I was little I would look for other ways of finding moths. One favourite was to turn on all the lights in my bedroom and open the windows. This results in you running manically around the place with a net to a pill box trying to make a capture or identify the mystery moth that just came buzzing in.

Above: *Garden tiger moth. Despite being blessed with funky markings, enough to put most butterflies to shame, these moths are, sadly, rarely seen, although common and widespread. The best way get a look at one is to try and lure one to a light.*

Below: *This common geometrid moth, the Magpie moth, is pretty widespread. It is found in woods and gardens.*

Left: *Homemade moth traps are worth trying, whether just a light bulb outside or a more complex trap that means you do not need to wait up. But the best and safest are purpose-built ones.*

Making your moth trap

You can make your own moth trap for about £15–20. But before you do, if you are a young person get an adult to help you out, because this does involve running electricity outside and with this there is an inherent risk of moisture – the combination of these two can kill. So be sure, be careful and always use a circuit breaker.

The basic idea is to construct a box, which has a removable lid, a funnel and a light above to lure in the moths.

Here is a basic version which works well enough. I've been a bit vague with the measurements, because they depend so much on the size of your bucket, but what does matter is that the bulb is suspended clear of the trap. You must make sure that it is protected from the rain (electricity and water are very dangerous together) and the whole construction should stick into the ground far enough to be stable.

You will need:
- *Plastic bucket*
- *meat skewer*
- *Candle*
- *Large sheet of clear plastic (approximately 70 cm x 70 cm depending on the size of your bucket)*
- *Strong glue*
- *Scissors*
- *Long flex*
- *Light bulb*
- *Plug*
- *Light bulb mount*
- *cable clips*
- *Three strips of wood, 2 cm x 2 cm in cross section (to make a frame to stick in the ground by 10 cm and suspend the light bulb at least 10 cm above the rim of the bucket)*
- *circuit breaker*
- *Small sheet of clear plastic (20 cm x 20 cm)*
- *egg boxes*
- *A piece of wood 10 cm x 10 cm x 1 m*
- *cloth tape*

1 Take the plastic bucket. Use the meat skewer, its tip heated in the candle flame, to punch some holes in the bottom of the bucket. These are for drainage.

2 Take the large piece of clear plastic and make it into a big funnel that sits in the top of the bucket. Use the glue to hold it together and the scissors to trim it to the ideal size and shape. It shouldn't be too deep in the bucket and the hole shouldn't be so small the moths do not fall in, nor so large they can escape. Place the funnel in the bucket, and trim the top so it just sticks out of the top by about 2 cm. You have now made the trap of the device.

3 Take the three pieces of wood and screw them together to make a shape like a football goal post. This must be 20 cm above the bucket's rim, when pushed into the ground, to allow for the bulb, its mount and a space of around 10 cm between the bulb and bucket rim.

4 Sharpen the ends that are due to be in the ground, use a saw or a file to point the ends that go in the ground.

5 Wire the flex to the plug and the bulb mount. Screw the light bulb mount to the flat piece of wood and attach this to the underside of the centre of the 'goal post' affair. Tidy up the flex with the cable clips.

6 Take the smaller piece of clear plastic and screw this to the top of the structure; this will act as an umbrella for the whole device, keeping rain out of the trap and off the light bulb.

7 That is all the hard stuff done. Now choose your spot, on soft ground and near to a power point for electricity. Place a few old egg boxes in the bucket, rest funnel in the bucket, place the 'goal post' with the bulb attached so it straddles the bucket. Push the posts into the ground so they are firm and do not wobble too much. Run the wire with the plug to the power point and make sure a circuit breaker is plugged in too, for your safety.

8 Wait until dusk and switch the light on. Leave this up and running all night. In the morning turn off all electricity and unplug the flex. Lift off the light bulb and goal post – be careful the light bulb may be hot.

9 Take the bucket and its contents to a shady place. Slowly remove the egg boxes and, with a good field guide, begin to identify the insects that you lured in. You will find that the types of moths and numbers caught will vary a lot depending on the time of the year and the weather. On warm, sticky, cloudy nights in the summer, a catch of hundreds is not a rare thing!

Orange tip butterflies

One butterfly that isn't hard to locate and is particularly entomologist friendly is the tangerine-tinged early spring butterfly the Orange tip. Only the males stand out and are instantly recognised by the bright orange tips to their forewings. As soon as you see these spring beauties on the wing, grab a field guide to British flowers and look up Cuckoo flower, Ladies smock or Milkmaid (different names for the same plant) and the closely related Hedge mustard. It does help to be a bit of a botanist in this game. Then simply get out there and find some. They usually flower the same time as the Orange tips are flying. This is no accident. Cuckoo flower and Hedge mustard are the main food plants of these insects and they are tied to the short flowering period in the spring because the caterpillars feed on the seed pods and young leaves of the plants.

The trick now is simply to start looking for the eggs. Look carefully at the underside of the flowers and their buds, and while most butterfly eggs try not to draw too much attention to themselves, the single spindle-shaped eggs of this species are, for some wonderfully mysterious reason, the same outrageous shade of orange as the males' forewings! A few weeks into the flying season of this insect, you will also stumble upon the signs that something has been chewing on some of the seed pods. This is an indication that some of the caterpillars have hatched. Look carefully to find them lying along the edges of the seed pods.

This becomes an addictive pastime and you will want to search for this welcome sign of spring every year on the first appearance of the adult insects.

Keeping and culturing

One way of really getting to know these bizarre beasts and the secret chapters of their lives, is to rear them through the stages to the adult insects. I think that everyone should at least have witnessed the emergence of a butterfly from its chrysalis before they die – with the right species it is easy.

To get going you need a few basic bits of kit and the animals themselves. You can't just go into your local pet shop and pick up half a dozen caterpillars, but there are specialised breeders all around the country and if that fails then you can collect your own using anyone of the masses of tips given in this book.

Horses for courses
With 60 regularly occurring British butterflies and the 800 or so large moths, there is a lot to choose from! But there are a few that are ideal to start with. These will provide spectacle, not be too fussy or have a common food

Right: *Look for Orange tip butterflies in your garden in early spring.*

plant. What is more, they are likely to succeed and not cause disappointment.

Food plant availability is first priority. It's no good getting an exotic, funky moth, that needs to feed on an equally exotic, funky plant. So choose carefully. I also like the idea of rearing a species that you have found yourself in your own patch. This means you have the right food plant nearby and that if you are a little bit successful with keeping them and end up with a shed or bedroom bursting with too many beautiful creatures, then you are not committing a crime by releasing a few back into the wild. (By the way many people at this stage get crazy conservation ideas and think that by rearing a species and releasing it into the wild they are helping – they are not. Trust me on this one, releasing a few will not hurt and the insects will live a natural life, but it isn't going to help the species in the long run.)

Below: *Around from April to September, Holly blue butterflies are fairly common in gardens and parks. You can also see them in hedgerows and at the edge of woodlands.*

Fresh eggs

Once you have obtained the eggs of either a butterfly or moth, keep them in a small airtight plastic box to protect them from predators, and to stop them drying out. You do not need to make air holes, there is enough for many days in the box, but it is still a good idea to open the box to ventilate and breathe on the eggs gently (to keep them moist) every other day.

Then it is simply a case of waiting and watching for a clue to the caterpillars' hatching. They often do this at night, so check every morning. Keep the box at room temperature and do not leave it in sunlight.

Hatch and go

One morning you will be rewarded with the sight of tiny caterpillars only a couple of millimetres long. These little chaps shouldn't be rushed off their eggs, as some need the first meal of the egg shell to start them off. Wait until they have wandered away from the eggs in search of food then, using a fine camel hair brush and a spoon, gently transfer them to another slightly bigger plastic box, lined with tissue paper and with a fresh leaf or two of the food plant (do not choose the newest shoots, or the tough leathery leaves, these either give them a bad stomach or are too tough to chew). Do not be tempted to put the caterpillars in too large a container as they will often wander off their food, get lost, get hungry and die. The perfect containers are very small margarine tubs, but make sure that they have been well washed out. At this stage do not worry about air holes, the caterpillars will only escape.

Keep checking the eggs until all have hatched. From now on the priority is to keep the food fresh and plentiful. Scrupulous daily cleaning is essential.

All is well when the caterpillars' dusty little droppings known as frass appear on the tissue paper.

All change

After a couple of days, the caterpillars will shed their skins for the first time. They often change colour at this stage and even though this is quite hard to see when they are so small, they spin themselves a little pad of silk to which they attach their back legs, this enables them to walk out of their old skin – the caterpillar equivalent of standing on the leg of your jeans while you pull the other leg out! When waiting to moult the caterpillars will appear very still. When they get bigger there is also a bulge just behind the head capsule. Do not disturb them at this stage, simply place the old leaves on some fresh ones. The caterpillars that are hungry will move; those moulting will do so when they are ready. Once the caterpillars have crawled out of their old skin they will resume feeding.

Growing up

After a week or so you will probably want to re-house your beasts, as they will be growing fast and producing more and more frass. They will start to produce more moisture themselves, which means it is time to increase ventilation. The next suitable house can be a bigger margarine pot, or a stout cardboard box such as a shoe box. *See panel below.*

Making your caterpillar box

1 Simply cut a hole in the lid, so the edges make a frame and then glue or staple a fine mesh, gauze or muslin, over this, making sure the holes are not big enough to let the caterpillars through – nobody, especially the animals themselves like free ranging!

2 Cut stems of the food plant can be placed in a small bottle or jar of water. Film canisters or paste bottles suffice in this respect as they are conveniently small and it is fairly easy to cut a hole in the lid for the plant stems. A final precaution to prevent the caterpillars from drowning is to stuff tissue paper or Plasticine in the gap around the stem.

3 As they grow continue to clean and refresh the food on a daily basis. If necessary upgrade to a bigger box.

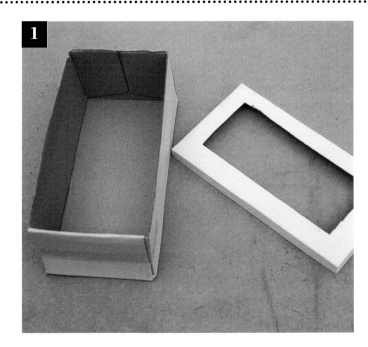

Re-mould and reshape

After five or so skin changes your caterpillars should be getting towards the end of their growing up. Many species will, just prior to moulting for the last time into the pupa, get an uncontrollable wanderlust – they often change colour at this point and go charging around the cage paying no attention to feeding. You must make sure at this stage you provide the right conditions for them to form a chrysalis or pupa.

Most butterflies need sticks or twigs on which they can dangle or brace themselves against. But moths, depending on species, often need either some egg boxes or a layer of soil in the bottom of their cage. The general rule is hairy caterpillars need egg boxes and smooth ones need soil, but there are exceptions to this.

If you are using soil make sure it is sterilised, I usually give it a blast for 10 minutes in the microwave. This kills any fungus, predators or diseases that may be lurking within. Let it cool and dampen it down with water again before placing in the bottom of your rearing cage. Big caterpillars like hawk moths will need quite a deep layer of soil at least 10-15 cm deep.

Playing the waiting game

The pupa or chrysalis now needs looking after. This is the bit where you give an inanimate object love and care and, for now at least, it gives you nothing back. This is the waiting stage.

In the wild this stage can last for anything from a few weeks to months, depending on the species' annual cycle and often the temperature the pupae are kept at.

Your chrysalis or pupae should now be placed in an emergence cage. This has to be spacious and well ventilated with branches, twigs or netting for the emerging adult to climb up.

Spray with water every few days, using a plant spray and keep the pupae out of the way of predators, especially when storing for the winter.

Above: *A night flyer, the Leopard moth occurs in gardens, parks and woodlands.*

A star is born

Eventually your prizes will emerge. The pupa or chrysalis darkens in colour, then goes semi-transparent – sometimes so much so you can see the patterns of the wings through its shell. Now is the time to keep checking back every few hours, especially during the early morning, a little survival mechanism to give the adult butterfly or moth time to crawl to safety and dry their wings under the cover of darkness. Having completed the cycle, the adults can now be released back into the wild or if you have a pair of moths then you can keep them and see if you can go around again by getting them to mate.

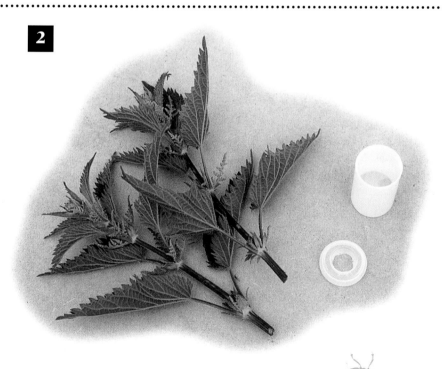

Field guide to common butterflies and moths

Large white

Small white

Small tortoiseshell

Peacock

Red admiral

Large and Small white butterflies

Large and Small white butterflies are collectively referred to as Cabbage whites because they, no surprises here, are rather fond of cabbages and plants in that family. They are common and are even considered a bit of a pest by gardeners, but they make fantastic subjects of study.

They both get confused as adults, but as caterpillars they live very different lives. Large whites are the butterflies I first reared as a child and I remember eagerly searching out the cabbages and another favourite food of theirs, nasturtiums, for the little rows of black-speckled caterpillars and clusters of bright yellow eggs, on the undersides of the leaves. These caterpillars remove nasty chemicals from the plants on which they feed and they keep them to use themselves. This means to predators such as birds that they would taste terrible, because of this chemical confidence they band together and are coloured in bright yellow, white and black as a warning.

They do, however, suffer from a parasitic wasp called *Apanteles*, which lays its eggs in the tissues of the caterpillar. So having your own poison isn't always the answer.

Large whites are common in the south, but less so in Scotland and Ireland. The Small white has roughly the same distribution as the Large white but is a much shyer creature. The eggs are laid singly on the underside of cabbage leaves and the green caterpillar skulks around in the folds of the cabbage, trying not to attract attention to itself. It doesn't go in for the chemical security of its bigger cousin.

Small tortoiseshell and Peacock butterflies

Small tortoiseshell and Peacock butterflies both feed on nettles. They are among the most common and widespread of our butterflies and you are bound to see them in your garden. Both species often hibernate in buildings

Poplar hawk moth

Lime hawk moth

Eyed hawk moth

Emperor moth

and garden sheds in late summer, coming out during mild winter spells.

The best way to collect stock of these is to look for the egg-laying adults in spring. But failing this, get out and look in a sunny nettle patch for nibbled nettles draped with silk. The earlier you collect your caterpillars (do not collect all of the batch, just take 15–20), the more likely you are to have success as they are plagued by a species of parasitic wasp and tiny parasitic fly.

Red admiral

The Red admiral is another common nettle butterfly that migrates to the UK every year from southern Europe. Its caterpillars are best found by searching the nettle bed for leaves that have been folded into a tent (not rolled, these usually belong to the shiny green caterpillar of the Mother-of-pearl moth, a species worthy of rearing in its own right).

As you get more experienced, you can try rearing other species, but I recommend getting a book or two on the subject first for more technical advice.

The moths are also good fun to rear, some of the easiest and most spectacular are the larger ones.

Lime, Eyed and Poplar hawk moths

Lime, Eyed and Poplar hawk moths are good to start with, especially as the adult moths do not feed, which cuts out one of the most difficult bits of breeding butterflies and moths, which is feeding them!

Emperor moth

Another bold choice, especially if you live near heathland, is the Emperor moth, Britain's only member of the silk moth family. The green caterpillars can be seen on Heather, brambles and other plants. These can be purchased from one of the UK's many livestock suppliers.

Dragonflies and Damselflies – 'Here there be Dragons'

Dragonflies were once referred to as 'horse stingers' or 'Devil's darning needles'; great names but don't think that these insects are rather nasty pieces of work that sting – they do not!

Dragonflies' extrovert tendencies, the fact that there are relatively few species in this country (38 species regularly breeding in Great Britain and Ireland) and that they are quite big, makes them fairly easy to get to grips with. The catch is that most are fairly fast fliers. The larger dragonflies can reach speeds of 36 kph (even damselflies can reach 10 kph), which makes following them with the eye next to impossible.

The hardware

Here comes their technical name – scientists refer to dragonflies as a group as the *Odonata* meaning 'toothed jaws', which gives away their game. These insects are not simply dainty, pretty things flitting around for our delectation. They are the winged assassins of all other

Below: *Do not expect dragonflies to stay in one spot as long as this hawker! The rare treat I'm experiencing here is down to cold air and the fact that this is a newly emerged insect.*

small insects and even the tiniest of damselflies is a ruthless murderer of midges – some even consume up to 20% of their own body weight a day.

At all stages of their lifecycle (other than the egg!) dragonflies and damselflies are totally carnivorous.

As nymphs (larvae) they are masters of ambush, lying in wait; some in the mud and leaves on the bottom of ponds, others amongst the water weeds. Their secret weapon is that they possess one of the most complex hunting gadgets – a set of extendible jaws or, strictly speaking, a lethal lower lip.

This deadly device is hinged under the head and when the nymph sees potential dinner (a passing tadpole, fish or other nymph), it extends the arm-like lip and stabs, grabs or spears the prey so fast that the action cannot be followed with the naked eye.

But evil though these little boggle-eyed aquatic aliens may appear, it is the jaws of the adult which gave rise to the family name *Odonata*.

Telling them apart

As a group of insects dragonflies are unmistakable: four large wings, large eyes, and long colourful body. It's telling apart the two groups – damselflies and dragonflies – that some people have trouble with.

The easiest way to distinguish between damselflies and dragonflies is by imagining a little scene. It's the one before the knight in shining armour turns up and rescues the fair maiden from the beastly dragon. The dragonflies, like their namesake in legend, are big, bold with an aggressive direct flight. Damselflies are smaller, more gentle, and their floppy flight is reminiscent of the fluttering handkerchief of the damsel in distress. Of course, there are lots more technical differences between the two but I

Body design

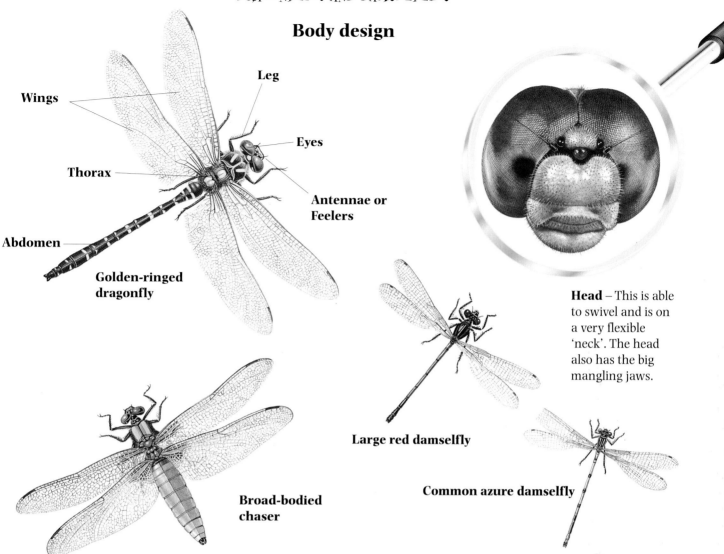

Wings

Leg

Eyes

Thorax

Antennae or Feelers

Abdomen

Golden-ringed dragonfly

Head – This is able to swivel and is on a very flexible 'neck'. The head also has the big mangling jaws.

Large red damselfly

Broad-bodied chaser

Common azure damselfly

always find that for beginners that little story helps identify the 'jizz' or overall feeling the insect portrays.

Incidentally, the name dragonflies is also used by scientists to describe both groups! So if in doubt call 'em dragonflies and you'll always be right.

The double life of a dragonfly

Size

As a general rule, dragonflies are bigger than damselflies. This rule works well in Great Britain, although in other parts of the world this isn't always the case.

Wings

They have two pairs of wings that in flight can be used independently of each other, giving them the agility and appearance of a helicopter, enabling them to hover, achieve vertical take off and landing and fly backwards. At rest, dragonflies hold their wings flat, while damselflies often rest with their wings folded up over their backs.

Eyes

Both insects are big on seeing– they have the biggest eyes of any insect. They have big boggly compound eyes that take up most of the space on their head. The eyes are made up of up to 28,000 tiny simple eyes all clustered together. Both insects have very good colour vision. They need to be able to see well to catch insects in flight. The dark bit in the middle is called a pseudopupil and is the area of the eye that can see the best.

Antennae or feelers

Because they spend most of their time flying and are rarely in contact with a hard surface, dragonflies and damselflies do not need feelers to feel. Instead they are very visual creatures with their antennae reduced to what look like tiny car radio aerials.

Thorax

Because dragonflies have to experience incredible forces through their wings when in flight, they need big and

87

The stick trick

Dragonflies and damselflies can be terribly unhelpful when you want to watch them, often perching way out over the water on lily pads, overhanging trees and other hard to get to places.

This little trick plays on the highly territorial behaviour of male damsel and dragonflies. It also allows you to bring the insects to you. All you need is a stick (a bamboo cane or a pea pole), binoculars and patience. The more sticks you set up the higher your chances of success. Simply find a body of water with plenty of dragon and damselfly activity. Choose a sunny summer's day and a bank which is sparse in tall natural vegetation and stick your stick into the bank or mud – ideally leaning slightly away from the bank and out over the water. This means that any dragonflies that use your perch will always be with their backs to you, making it easier to look at their colours and wings. Then it is simply a case of sitting, watching and waiting.

powerful muscles to work them and row through the air, hence a big engine box of a thorax.

Legs

The six legs all stick forward from the dragonfly's body and each one is covered in big spine-like bristles. This makes them okay for perching and useless for walking, but when held together on the wing they become a death trap. They work just like a butterfly net, enabling the predator to scoop up and catch other small insects in flight.

Abdomen

This contains all the organs that the dragonfly needs for digestion and breeding. It is also the most colourful part of the body and the colours and patterns are essential for identification. Females tend to be different colours and patterns from the males and not quite as gaudily decked out.

Be careful in your identification of immature adults as these can often be a different colour from the fully mature adults all together – now you can see why a good field guide is essential!

The secret life of the dragonfly

1 Their favourite position for mating is the wheel. The male is gripping the female behind her head. She curls her abdomen up to the base of his.
2 Egg laying can often be observed on a warm sunny day; different species use different techniques. Some lay inside plant stems, others dip their abdomens in flight, directly into the water, releasing clouds of eggs. Others lay carefully on submerged weeds.
3 The nymph spends up to a couple of years under the water, growing and living like the voracious predator it is. Dragonflies breathe through the gills inside their bottoms. Damselflies have feathery external gills.
4 The transition from the water world to the wing, occurs usually during the early morning. The nymph crawls up vegetation and splits its nymphal case to emerge, a pale and soft adult insect, with crumpled wings.
5 Now we see the fully primed, expanded and coloured up adult insect, ready to start zooming about murdering flies!

Behaviour to look out for

Egg laying

Different species use different egg laying techniques. The most obvious egg laying behaviour is 'stabbing', when the females of Darter and Emerald dragonflies can be seen 'pogoing' across the pond, appearing to be bouncing on the tip of their abdomens. The simple dipping action of the female's abdomen washes the eggs off and they slowly sink below the surface.

Other methods of dispersing eggs are carried out actually inside the tissue of pond plants, by cutting a small slit in the plant and inserting the individual egg. This is what is happening when you see the insect resting on the vegetation and probing around with the tip of their abdomen. Some female damselflies even drag themselves completely under water down the plant stem and what's more they often pull their mate too, still attached by his claspers!

Territorial dog fights

Dragonflies and damselflies, in particular the males, can be aggressive and very possessive of a territory. Their

Jet demo

If you gently lift a hawker dragonfly nymph to the surface of the water with your finger and hold it with its bottom just clear of the surface you can actually see it squirt a jet of water in the air as it tries to escape from you!

only goal is to ensure they mate with and fertilise as many females as possible.

The females wander widely as they mature and feed themselves up, but sooner or later they have to return to the water and here the males are waiting. Males find a good perch to survey as much of the water as possible (see *The stick trick*). They will chase and try to impress the girls when they arrive and some of the chases you see will be of this kind.

But other males of the same species have the same plan, this means the sky over the pond or river becomes a battle zone during the height of summer, with males trying to drive other males away in spectacular aerial dog fights, with lots of chasing and clashing of wings.

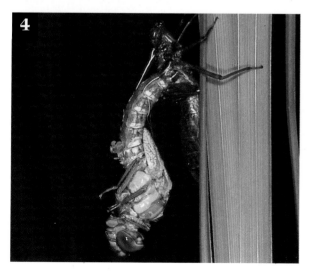

Body design – damselfly nymph

Big eyes – Just like the adult insects, the nymphs hunt their prey by sight and need big eyes too.

Size and shape – Size is very variable, depending on what moult you are looking at. Shape is a more useful indication. While dragonflies come in different shapes varying from short, fat and flat to long and torpedo-like, damselflies are nearly always long and almost spidery in appearance.

Gills – This is easily the best means of identification. If it has what looks like three feathers sticking out of its back end then it is almost certainly a damselfly. These are the gills. Look at the head as well because mayfly nymphs also have three gills, but a different look to their head and eye arrangement. Dragonflies have gills in a hollow in their abdomen and so by strict definition are able to breathe through their bottom.

Wing buds – Look carefully at your nymph and if it is a later moult, the chances are it has very obvious wing buds on its back.

Jaws – Owners of the meanest gnashers in the pond, both dragonflies and damselflies have some complicated mouthparts that they can shoot out and forward, catching their victim by surprise.

Mating

This can appear to be rather confusing in most species as they adopt a strange position known as the wheel. Go down to any duck pond in the summer and you will see some damselflies joined together in tandem.

The male, just before mating, pops his sperm from the tip of his abdomen into a special pouch right at the other end of his abdomen on the underside of the second segment. When a pair meet up and like the look of each other, the male grasps the female's neck with a pair of finger-like projections on the tip of his bottom, called claspers. Then she reaches forward with her abdomen to get the sperm stored in the male's special pouch – this results in the wheel position. Impressed? Well, some of the damselflies can maintain this for over six hours! And even fly around in this position.

Exuviae

Look around the edges of ponds and streams in the summer at any emergent vegetation (that is technical talk for plants that are sticking out of the water). You may notice the empty old nymphal cases of dragonflies and damselflies. They are called exuviae and look like hollow nymphs – goggly eyes and all! They get a bit crispy and fragile, but you can collect them and glue or pin them on to a bit of polystyrene or cardboard. You can soak the skin in water to make it less brittle and, using a needle or pin, tease out that extendible jaw.

Feeding

Adult damselflies and dragonflies catch their food on the wing using their special basket-like legs, but occasionally you will find one that has caught a large insect and it will take this sizeable meal to a favourite perch to eat it.

Hunting is carried out in a systematic way. Some fly up and down over the water, others can be seen flying backwards and forwards, quartering woodland rides and skimming the tops of low-growing plants. Others rest on their perch and pounce on insects, returning to the perch seconds later to eat and wait again.

Dragon hunting – getting started

The avid dragon and damsel watcher needs a few bits of equipment. A pair of close focus binoculars are very handy, because a lot of the action takes place in the middle of the pond or river and it is nice to see what they get up to and identify them. A magnifying lens is essential for looking at nymphs and empty skins close up.

Pond nets are useful for reaching into the water, to collect and find nymphs. A butterfly net, which is lighter than a pond net, can be useful, but handling dragonflies without hurting them requires skill and patience and is really for experts and real dragonfly nuts. I find I can get by without one and I recommend that you do too.

If you are looking in the water for nymphs, several clear pots are essential if you want to really appreciate what monsters these young insects are. A white tray for sorting these sometimes very camouflaged animals out from the weed, mud and gravel is handy too. A good field guide will help you to put names to everything you find, although a few hours watching these animals is still an experience in itself.

Experiment: Hatching your own

Choose a still-water habitat as it is easier to provide for the needs of the nymphs than for those that live in fast-flowing streams. Set up a fish tank with no lid in a light spot, out of direct sunlight (outside is best so that the insects will be free to fly away). Fill it with clean rain/pond water and add pond weed and small pond life. Add a few branches sticking out for the insects to crawl up.

Remember you only need 2 or 3 large specimens for a fish tank about 50–60 cm long. Look at the wing buds; they are a good indication of age. Those with longer wings are more likely to hatch during the season.

Above: *A favourite pastime for me since I was knee high to a grasshopper is pond dipping. A good sturdy net with a handle is all that is required to find the nymphs.*

Feed your nymphs on small worms. When they are about to change into an adult they hang around near the surface as their gills stop working and they start breathing like the adult insect – through tiny holes in their thorax called spiracles. Now keep an eye open for the grand finale! It usually happens in the early morning or evening so watch closely at these times of the day.

If you are lucky you may witness what has to be one of the most beautiful sights in the insect world. Following its laboured crawl up the stems, the nymph splits open along a natural weak spot at the back of its head and a brand new dragonfly oozes out of the husk (see *Exuviae*).

If you are unlucky and you miss the emergence don't worry, try again (it took me five attempts before I got lucky!). On the bright side you are left with a souvenir – the nymph has left you its old skin.

Crickets and Grasshoppers – The Frenetic Fiddlers

Few habitats don't hum, scratch and buzz to the tune of these insects in the summer. Most make themselves known by sound alone. They are often well hidden in the undergrowth or in a sward of grass. Some have an uncanny ability to throw their 'voices' so even when you think you should be getting close, the chirping always seems to be coming from the next clump of grass!

You know about grasshopper's jumping legs and that they use them to produce sound somehow. But this group contains beastly predators and gentle vegetarians, masters of disguise, and some of the loudest shouters in the British countryside, so I'm sure you will want to get to know them better.

It's simply not cricket: telling them apart

There are 30 species in the British Isles, which makes it quite easy to get your head around this group of insects. But they are all very good at hiding, so to say they are not challenging would be a big lie.

Above: *A good place to start looking for grasshoppers and crickets is, you guessed it, in the grass!*

As a group they are very diverse in appearance, some are small and look like stones, others do great impressions of plants, some fly, others don't. So what feature makes them stand out from other insects?

Scientists argue about exactly what to call them. Some say *Orthoptera*, which means straight-winged; others say *Saltatoria*, which comes from the Greek word that means to jump. Grasshoppers and crickets are famous for jumping and to perform this act they all have big back legs, to ping themselves through the air.

Now we have sorted that one out, it is time to separate the crickets from the grasshoppers, which is really easy.

Antennae

These two structures are the quickest way to separate them. Crickets have wispy, whip-like antennae, which are longer than the body. Grasshoppers have very short much thicker antennae. The reason for the difference is probably that crickets are nocturnal and need longer antennae to feel their way around and find food.

Ears

Because sound is important to their lives, used in communication and for finding a mate, crickets and grasshoppers have 'ears' – not the kind you find on the side of your head but similar in principle to the ear drum. They are called tympanal organs and in crickets they are found on the front pair of legs. In grasshoppers their 'ears' are at the base and sides of their abdomen, but don't bother looking as they are nearly always hidden by the wings and are tricky to see, even at the best of times.

Legs

They both have the usual complement of six, as grasshoppers and crickets are insects; the last pair are larger and contain strong muscles that generate the jumping force. The front pair of legs in crickets contain an 'ear' on each leg just below the knee and in bush

Body design

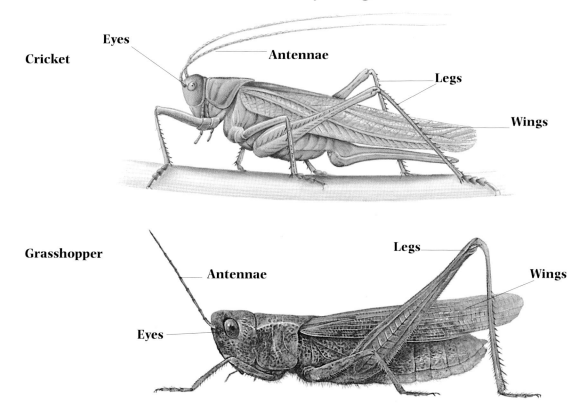

Cricket — Eyes, Antennae, Legs, Wings

Grasshopper — Antennae, Legs, Wings, Eyes

crickets they are armed with lots of spines and spikes, which are used in a similar way to those of a praying mantis – to strike and pin down smaller prey insects.

Mouthparts
The main jaws are like a big set of secateurs or meat shears, and are perfect tools for mashing up both plants and animals, the palps either side are used for feeling and tasting the food.

Wings
A thin pair of pleated and folded frail hind wings are hidden behind and protected by a pair of leathery forewings.

Left: *Looking like an alien, a cricket's mouthparts are just as ferocious as they look.*

Making cricket tongs

During the warmer months it is not hard to find the green nymphs of Speckled bush crickets and the brown young of Dark bush crickets, sitting still in bramble patches. Try and catch them though and you often get yourself snagged up. One false move, the bush tremors and before you can say 'Blasted blackberries!' the cricket has hopped it!

The answer to your troubles lies in a long pair of scissor-like barbecue tongs, but not as they come! This would lead to a nasty squishing! Using strong cloth duck tape, attach a pair of tea strainers to the end of each half of the tongs, so that they close together to form a little mesh cage. With this you should be able to bag crickets, grasshoppers and many other nervous insects for that matter.

93

Stridulating organs – the bits that make the noise
Grasshoppers fiddle using their hindlegs as a bow, rubbing a set of pegs on the inside of the thick bit of the leg against a raised vein on the forewing.

Crickets make their noise by rubbing a serrated rib of one wing against the rib of another wing. There is a clear, roundish area on the wing called a mirror, which is used to amplify the sound.

The call of the Oak bush cricket is made by vibrating one of its rear feet against the surface of the leaf on which it sits. The large Marsh grasshopper kicks its wings with the spines on its back legs, making a popping sound.

Ovipositor
This is the posh name for the egg-laying tube and it is this which gives crickets their technical name of *Ensifera*, from the Greek word meaning sword-shaped. You can see this in most female crickets, even young ones, and it is a good way of sexing them. Grasshoppers have smaller and less well defined appendages and it's a lot harder to tell male from female.

Grassroots symphony

Why do crickets and grasshoppers sing? Well, it's a good question, but I guess the answer is something to do with the kind of place they live. Dense vegetation and the fact that they all like hiding from predators makes finding your mate a hard job. Like small song birds, crickets and

Below: *Grasshoppers chirp by rubbing one leg against their forewing, rather like a violinist rubbing the bow against his violin. Look closely on the inside of the thick part of a grasshopper's leg and you will see a set of pegs. These are rubbed against a raised vein on the forewing.*

Coneheads – out of range

Most of these songs are well within the audible range of a human being but if you are an adult listening for the songs of coneheads, a kind of bush cricket, then be prepared to feel old. As we grow our ears lose a little of their ability. I'm not talking ancient here; from their early thirties onwards most adults cannot hear the frequencies this insect's song is in, but their children will!

grasshoppers sing to attract females and to establish their territories.

It is usually the males that make all the cacophony. The females are generally mute, although some species make a quiet delicate little squeak, to entice the males.

Each species can be identified by its calls, a serenade call for the ladies, a war cry when they come across a rival male and fight and then a territory song, which is saying 'Keep out of my patch!'

Perfect miniatures

Grasshoppers and crickets have an incomplete lifecycle, that is they do not live a four-stage saga, like the butterflies and beetles. They start off as an egg and then go through a series of moults that, from hatching to the final product, are recognisable as the adult insect.

Below: *Crickets chirp by rubbing grooves on one wing vein against similar grooves on the veins of the other wing. They then amplify this scratchy chorus by lifting their wings to form a loudhailer affair and also by a device called a mirror in the wing surface.*

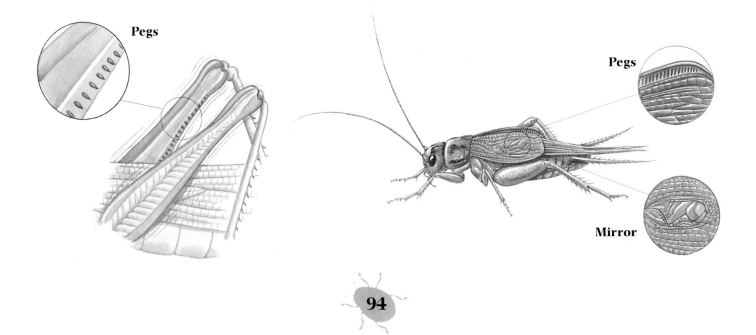

Pegs

Pegs

Mirror

Bush cricket lifecycle

1 The lifecycle of crickets and grasshoppers is very similar and is known as incomplete, because it does not have larval or pupal stages. First they over winter as an egg.

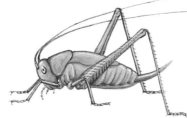

2 On hatching from the egg, these insects look like miniature adults, but their sexual apparatus and wings are not fully developed.

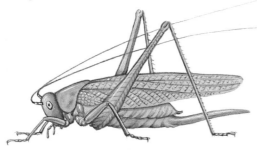

3 They go through a number of skin sheds until they reach adulthood.

Above: *Common field grasshopper. Run through long grass in the summer and you are almost certain to send this species jumping. It is one of the commonest grasshoppers and lends its chirping to the sound track of summer.*

4 In most species adulthood is marked by fully formed wings.

It is not uncommon to stumble across these perfect miniatures in spring and early summer. The clue as to the age of the insect comes from the size of the wing buds or pads, which you can see if you look at the insect's back. Only fully grown adults have fully developed wings. These are normally but not always as long or longer than the insect's body.

Rearing nymphs

One of the best ways to see these stages is to rear a few nymphs. This can be achieved very easily by keeping the nymphs in a plastic aquarium with a fine netting on the top. Don't leave the tank on a sunny window ledge – the sun will soon fry the inhabitants. Instead the desired effect can be achieved with a 60 watt bulb, mounted on the inside of the tank, or a desk lamp held over the set up. Place the lamp on a timer switch, allowing the same sort of daylight time as is occurring in the wild.

Grasshoppers can be fed a varied grass diet, either freshly cut or planted in soil. I prefer the freshly cut method as it reduces the risk of predators getting in with

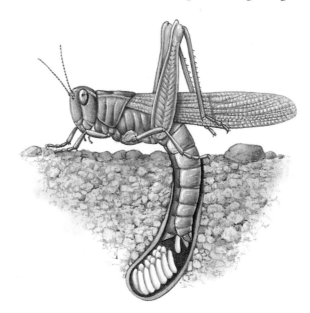

Above: *Grasshopper laying eggs. Unlike crickets, female grasshoppers do not have long egg laying tubes. Instead they have a very flexible abdomen. The tissues between the segments are some of the stretchiest in the animal kingdom and allow the clutch of eggs to be laid deep in the soil.*

the grass. Tie a small bundle of mixed grasses together on a piece of string. It can be lowered into the tank without the risk of any of your charges jumping out. Once the grasshoppers have sussed there is fresh food, they will move to it and the old bunch can be removed.

Crickets are much more omnivorous and need to be fed a very different diet. Give them plenty of variety: bread soaked in honey, grasses, flowers (a good source of protein), fish food flakes, fruit, live insects such as young grasshoppers and blowflies (easily obtainable from angling shops).

In both types of cage place some twiggy branches to give the insects something to cling onto when they moult. Watching the complex and leggy beast that is a grasshopper or cricket hang itself upside down, have its neck split open and a perfect pale and soft new-looking insect gently fall out of its old skeleton has to be seen to be believed, especially the moment when the antennae are pulled out with such force that you'll keep looking away convinced there will be a twanging sound as one of them breaks!

Depending on the species, they will shed their skin between four and ten times during their nymphal career before reaching adult size.

Although these animals easily lay eggs in the soil provided, and it is fascinating to see them do this, some species take several years to hatch and so this can make the keeping of them all the way through their life-cycle a bit of a challenge for all but the most dedicated grasshopper and cricket fan!

Cricket season – finding and catching them

It is all very well making lots of noise, but it does come with its disadvantages. If you sing to advertise your presence it isn't just the intended that are going to hear your call. There are lots of eavesdropping animals out there eager for a crunchy snack.

So to avoid being caught crickets and grasshoppers are good at pretending to be plants. Many use a combination of greens, browns and greys to blend into their backgrounds. Others, such as ground hoppers, do passable impressions of pebbles, while the conehead crickets rest up during the day, drawing their legs and antennae together and tucking in tight to plant leaves. Some simply hang out in the densest of vegetation and it can be very frustrating to hear the Great green bush cricket of your dreams singing its wings off from the centre of a

Living thermometers

Grasshoppers and crickets are, like all Arthropods, often referred to as being cold blooded. This means their activity patterns are often tied to the temperature of the surrounding environment.

A good way of demonstrating this is to listen to them. When their bodies are up around 30°C they are fully charged and can go about their business. Just listen to a field at the height of summer on a warm sunny day, the joint rocks with crickets and grasshoppers scratching, chirping and clicking all over the place. But go to the same meadow on a dull, overcast, typical summer day and it will seem like another place altogether, very quiet indeed.

Big bush crickets show this very well. Great green bush crickets have one of the loudest songs of any British insect and when it's a scorcher they will sing an almost continuous trill, but as the air temperature drops down to less than 15°C the individual chirps can be detected. You can test this by using the chirps of these and other bush crickets to tell the temperature.

What you do is, using a watch, count the number of chirps in 15 seconds and do this several times to

Above: *Dark bush cricket. An unlikely looking thermometer I think you will agree, but like many insects its activity is dependent on the temperature of its surroundings and this activity includes singing.*

get an average. Then, to find the air temperature in Celsius, divide this number by 2, then add 6. Your answer should be the temperature in Celsius within a couple of degrees. Now double check this with a thermometer.

How accurate is your species? Are other types more accurate? Now try it on grasshoppers, do you get any useful results?

bush and simply not being able to get close enough to see it!

Assuming you do eventually get close enough for a view it is so often met with a 'ping' and your quarry has put those famous jumping legs to good use and left the scene very quickly and efficiently.

If we want to study these animals we need to overcome all these defence strategies. Here are several little tricks for outwitting grasshoppers and crickets. Which trick you use depends on which species you are looking for.

Grasshoppers tend to live in grassy field edges, meadows and the like, and you can certainly home in on them by just their song. But for every one singing, you are probably missing out on the females, young nymphs and many other species. These can be swept for using a sweep net (see page 131), a net a bit like a butterfly net but with a stronger white cloth bag and a stout frame and handle. You can buy these or have a go at making one yourself. Sweep the net through long grass a couple of times and then investigate the bag – it normally isn't too long before you have found a grasshopper or two. Sweep different habitats and you will find different species.

Bush crickets tend to be a little trickier because they seem to prefer bushes or at least thicker vegetation nearby. For these you can use the beating tray technique (see page 71) or you can use a method known as 'walking up'. This is nothing more than walking along like a heron, keeping your eyes in the vegetation in front of your feet. After you have got your eye in you will be surprised at how easy it is. Soon you will be able to identify a species just by the way it jumps, flips or flops out of your way! I use it to locate the rough whereabouts of the insects by singing individual and then look for a bit of grassy habitat nearby to walk through. Another superb way to find them is to go out at night with a pair of peeled eyeballs and a torch – combine these with a pair of cricket tongs and you'll stand a chance.

Right: *The Oak bush cricket is not found only on oak trees. It is attracted to light, and can be lured using the beam of a torch.*

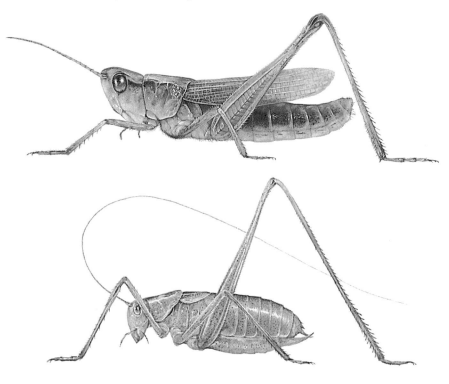

Above top: *The Meadow grasshopper is unusual in that it is unable to fly, the hindwings are vestigial.* Above bottom: *Speckled bush cricket – females as well as males sing.*

Shed light on a secret

Oak bush crickets are active at night so you rarely see them. They don't sing, but do a little tap dance with their rear legs so it's very hard to hear them. You can often find them by beating small bushes in the same way you find caterpillars. But another trick relies on their attraction to light. You can lure them down out of the leaves by strapping a powerful torch with long life batteries to the trunk of an oak tree, making sure the beam points up. Come back after it's been dark for a few hours and you could have one or two sitting in the beam.

Wasps – Striped Hunters with a Sweet Tooth

Do not fall into the mind trap that all wasps are yellow and black 'jobbies' out to get you. It simply isn't true and, besides, you are probably thinking of the eight social species found, which, like honey and bumble bees, consist of colonies of sisters founded by the mother. The majority of British species are solitary!

High society?

First we have to cut through wasps' reputation and answer the question that always comes up when I'm preaching the word of wasps and that is 'What good do wasps do?' My answer goes like this. Wasps are predators, feeding insects and the like to their developing grubs. Wasps will graze their way through a colony of greenfly in a couple of hours, a truly disgusting scene, but one that will please many gardeners in its ruthless efficiency!

Extra services provided by these yellow-jacketed janitors of the garden scene are that they hunt out caterpillars and many other harmful insects in the herbaceous border.

Sweet and sticky

Only the larvae eat flesh, the wasps themselves, like the adults of most *Hymenoptera* (see page 104), have a penchant for the sweet and sickly. Remember, one of the things we really like about bees is their service to flowers, whether fruit trees, vegetables or just the pretty ones in the border – wasps do all this too! In fact for the botanically interested, there is a cool flower called a Snake's-head fritillary which in Europe is mainly pollinated by social wasps.

Above: *A familiar sight in the autumn, as workers from the wasp nest go on a binge, having been released from their nest duties by the fading queen.*

Many of the tiny solitary wasps all perform beneficial services but because they do not have the advanced social societies of the yellow and black stripy ones they are not able to live in such a variety of habitats.

I think wasps get a raw deal from us, the ignorant human. A little sting, that is only rarely put on us, is a small price to pay for all their benefits. I am convinced if they didn't have that sting, we would all love these animals to bits!

Inside the wasp factory

Wasps have an annual cycle that starts in the spring with a single mated queen. Having overwintered, she sets out to found a colony, which by the end of the summer will be a bustling metropolis of insect activity with several thousand individuals milling around inside the paper nest. Some species nest underground and those that have exposed nests in trees and hedges are often hidden exceedingly well. Even if they are not, safe observation of their toing and froing can only be made at a distance with binoculars.

High rise flats

I find this frustrating as the nest construction and what goes on inside is mind-blowingly beautiful. Once I had a

98

Above: *When hibernating, queens take on a very distinctive posture, often gripping with the jaws. The legs and wings are folded up and sit in a groove along the side of her body. Most of these insects do not actually survive the winter; loads die of exposure, starvation or from being eaten by birds, rodents and spiders.*

bizarre opportunity to witness the inside of a living wasp nest that had been built up against a window; because the room was dark the wasps hadn't sealed the window side off.

Inside were several layers of cells like the floors in a block of flats, but upside down having been built and hung from the ceiling of the nest downwards. I could watch the larvae, stuffed into the cells like fat people in sleeping bags, being tended by worker wasps. Whenever the grubs wanted attention they scratched their mouth-parts on the sides of their cells, a noise I could hear, even through the glass.

The queen was only sometimes evident, gracing us with her swollen presence every now and then, but the workers were everywhere all at once. Some were build-ing and I watched as they flew backwards and forwards

Above: *If you find a wasp, slightly drunk from the nectar of a flower, grab your magnifying hand lens and take a good look at the amazing warning colours of their abdomen.*

Below: *Mature nest. If you want to witness the beauty of a nest without the threatening presence of thousands of workers, look around at the beginning of the year. Good places are in loft spaces and garden sheds. If you look close-ly you'll see that the cells inside are, in fact, hexagonal.*

Below: *A flying Common wasp, one of the most under-appreciated insects in the world.*

with mouths full of wood pulp, which they spat out and crafted with their jaws, every mouthful set and dried like papier maché.

Cool air system

At the entrance there was lots of activity; a stream of caterpillars and other insects being flown in and wasps were poised like sentinels on guard duty inside the door. But one of the most remarkable things to watch was the way these insects controlled the internal conditions of the nest.

As the day progressed, the sun moved around the sky and warmed things up inside. Some workers sat just in the entrance fanning their wings, to get cool air circulating; others fanned around inside pushing the warm air around further. As things got hotter, wasps made trips to a nearby birdbath to gather water. This they brought back to the nest and spat out on the walls and cells. In the same way as sweat evaporating from our skin cools us down, the evaporating water would keep the nest cool.

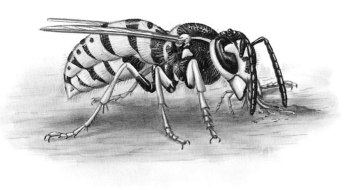

Above: *Wasp collecting wood pulp. The raw material for the carton nest of social wasps is wood and you may well notice the workers collecting thin shavings from garden furniture, gates and fence posts.*

Watching wasps

This was one of the entomological highlights of my career but it is a rare treat to see all this, the tender side of wasps. So as well as imagining what is going on in that hole under the garden shed, you can do a bit of detective work, keep your eyes peeled and you may well see some of this behaviour from the other end.

Look for wasps catching insects to take back to the nest. Watch around the edges of ponds, puddles and birdbaths on hot days for wasps gathering a belly full of water for the nest air conditioning system and look out on garden sheds and fence posts for worker wasps scraping a little pile of wood pulp together to build the nest.

Strange fruit – the embryo nest

A very fragile golf or tennis ball shaped thing, the new nest is usually creamy white to grey in colour, suspended from the ceiling. This could get to be a metre or more across in size by the end of the year!

When a nest is at this stage it is usually tended only by the queen, her first batch of daughters, having not yet grown up. She starts off doing everything herself, building the first cluster of brood cells and enclosing the entire thing in a fragile envelope of carton or wasp paper (wood pulp mixed with her saliva). She also feeds and incubates the grubs once they have hatched by curling her body around the base of the cells.

If you find one of these strange fruits, the first thing to do is ascertain whether or not the insect is in. Many nests are abandoned at this stage. The queen wasp decides she has made a duff decision in the nest's location, or she dies or is killed.

Close up on a nest

Because she has a lot on her plate and is busy, she may well be out foraging during the day. At night, however, she will return to her home. It is now you should gently approach the nest with a torch and try looking up into the nest through the entrance hole to see if she is in. If the nest is being used, sit and watch her at work during the day by simply sitting and waiting, keeping a diary of events. If, however, she has abandoned her first quarters, and you are sure she has not returned, you can collect the nest and examine it close up. Look for the different coloured bands of carton on the outside, each representing a different source of wood fibre.

Recycled paper

The remarkable thing about these nests is that, as it grows and expands the carton can be recycled, rewetted and remoulded into new shapes as the colony swells.

You can try cutting the envelope in half with scissors to show the brood cells and the structure inside.

Wrapping it up

The new queens to be and the males are released from the colony in late summer. This is the event the whole nest has been gearing up for and it is worth looking out for a behaviour known as hill topping. What happens is that the queens to be and the males all head for a local landmark. I have seen them gathering on the hills around Dartmoor, church spires, even tall hedges, walls and conifer trees. Here the queens and males meet.

House of ill repute

Back at the nest things start to change. The orderly, strictly functioning baby factory turns into a house of ill repute. The workers become those striped vagabonds that get lodged in your pint glass, your ice cream, your hair and clothes. These are not the perfect functioning worker wasps that worked so selflessly for their queen and colony just a month or so ago. The latter has become dysfunctional, the production line of wasp eggs, larvae and pupae has ground to a halt. The workers are unemployed, drowsy, disorganised and can be a plain nuisance to us.

Above: *This embryo wasp nest in a loft space is the work of one queen, but once her work force starts to emerge, the nest will grow beyond belief. Some measure a metre across and harbour several thousand individuals by late summer!*

The elderly queen is slowing down. Her influence over the workers is diluting. She's laying fewer eggs, so there are fewer workers to tend the larvae still in the cells. These larvae are weaker anyway because they have been feeding the males with their saliva prior to departure on their first and final fling.

A right royal mess

The means by which the queen had been holding reign is a chemical one – namely delta-n-hexadecalactone. This subdues the workers who pick it up while tending to her majesty. Without it the workers riot and fight (something that can be seen around nests). The chemical usually gets spread around the colony as worker feeds worker and more importantly as worker feeds grub! With fewer grubs and workers the orderly insect palace becomes a right royal mess.

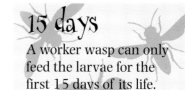

15 days
A worker wasp can only feed the larvae for the first 15 days of its life.

Above left: *Spangle galls. These capsules are created by a reaction of the plant tissues to the eggs and larvae of tiny wasps. On this leaf are two kinds – Common spangle galls at the top and Silk button galls below.*

Above right: *Artichoke galls. Another kind of gall produced by another gall wasp. Handily named for its resemblance to an artichoke!*

Going for galls

Galls are the tiny life support capsules for the grubs and pupae of little flies and wasps. These insects are so small that very few people actually see them alive, and yet these tiny architects produce all those wacky and 'gonzo' designs.

Look for artichoke galls (green and scaly, about the size of a medium sized marble) on oak twigs. Spangle galls are the little 'flying saucer' shaped discs found on the underside of old oak leaves around the bases of trees. Collect these and place them in a large clear plastic bag, inflated with a straw, with a plug of cotton wool or cloth in the entrance (for a little ventilation) tie shut

Below: *The Ruby-tail wasp. This little flying metallic masterpiece is a parasite on Mason bees and can often be seen searching for their nests on walls and fence posts.*

with string and wait for the little wasps (all females) to appear near the top of the bag. Some will hatch early due to temperature change but keep them cool and most will hatch in the spring.

If you want a more instant insight into the world of the gall wasp, look for the empty galls of Marble galls and Oak apples, then cut them in half and you will see what goes on inside.

Going it alone

Solitary wasps are very hard to identify, because they come from all sorts of different backgrounds and have a range of appearances. The one thing they have in common is that they are all hyperactive insects, that love sunny situations. The females work alone to construct a nest, usually a burrow or hollowed out plant stem and in it they place food in the form of an insect or spider, which is paralysed by the sting in order to keep the meat fresh for the grubs. The grubs hatch from eggs laid inside the cell.

An introduction to the most exciting of these insects is to find a warm sunny and sandy location: dunes, heaths and sunny path edges are good, and here you simply look for holes and winged activity.

Identification can be a bit of a minefield but that shouldn't stop your enjoyment of the show.

The frenetic *Ammophila sabulosa* is one of the largest solitary wasps. It is often called the sand wasp, because of its love of sandy soils in which to dig. These large

Above: *Marble gall. Again found on oaks, this is a very distinctive gall being large, round and smooth. Cut one open and you will see the chamber of the grub inside.*

black spindly wasps with the red/brown waist band can be seen digging their burrows, flying off with loads of excavated material, stoppering their burrows to deter squatters before returning with a paralysed caterpillar to stuff in the hole along with an egg.

If you sit still long enough you can watch the nesting process, including the circular, orientation flight as she leaves her nest site. This is when she takes in landmarks; like stones and plants and she will remember these so she can return home. Move a stone out of place and she will return confused, replace the stone and she will pick up from where she left off.

Other species often share the same colony location. Look out for black and yellow striped weevil hunters of the *Cerceris* genus, stocking their mini volcanoes with their beetle cargo. Another great one to look out for is one of the cuckoo wasps like the Ruby-tail wasp – *Chrysis* species – an animal whose low down and dirty ways (laying its eggs in the nests of others) is masked by its beautiful metallic red and blue garb.

The trackers

If you see an animal that looks a bit like a wasp, isn't a bee, has a waist, is predominantly dark in colour with a few bright white or yellow markings and it is twitching its antennae fervently, then it is probably one of the *Ichneumon* wasps. These insects always look like they are searching for something and their name means the tracker.

Ichneumon wasps do not make a nest. They are not even slightly social. They are parasites. Their larvae grow up inside other creatures.

There are absolutely loads of these insects, many with great names that seem to point towards their seedy, gruesome ways; names like the persuader and suspicious wasp.

Among the ones to look out for is the large and spidery Opium wasp. This often comes to light and I have found it on many occasions on a lit window or in my moth trap in the morning. It is spectacular and the females have a secret ovipositor which they use to place their eggs deep within the bodies of various moth caterpillars. Try to handle it with care because even though the ovipositor is not really a sting this is one of the bigger ichneumons and I have certainly felt a stinging sensation in my hand after capturing one to remove it from my moth trap.

Eaten alive!
Another closely related parasitic wasp is the tiny *Apanteles* wasp which commonly lays a load of eggs inside the caterpillars of Large white butterflies.

If you rear these from wild-caught stock, be prepared for some of them to be a little slow in their development and not as big, because this is a sure sign that inside their bodies a clutch of grubs are eating away at the flesh. The larvae of these wasps are smart in that they do not touch vital organs. They eat around the heart, nerves and breathing tubes, feasting on the fat and other tissues, so that their host keeps eating and living and they keep on growing inside.

Keep an eye on the big caterpillars, as one day like a scene from the film *Alien*, lots of maggot-like creatures burst forth through the unfortunate caterpillar's skin.

As the larvae settle down and spin their yellow silk cocoons around it, the caterpillar, although hollow and saggy, is often still alive, but will eventually collapse and die, with no energy to even leave the grisly scene. What started as a quick stabbing in the neck has turned, for this caterpillar, into a clip from a horror movie.

Below: *These larvae of parasitic wasps are emerging from this caterpillar where they have been slowly developing.*

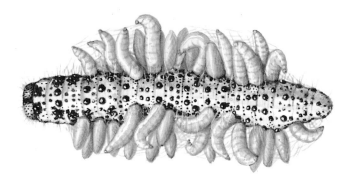

The Buzz about Bees

And you thought that a wasp was a wasp and a bee was a bee. Well, have I got a surprise for you! If you think all bees live in hives and make lots of honey for us, you couldn't be more wrong.

Above: *The hardest working insect, the Honey bee, will apparently visit 64 million flowers to make just 1 kg of honey! Hence busy as a bee, I guess.*
Left: *A useful piece of equipment, a bee box in a sunny position can attract many species of solitary bee to your garden (see* Making your bee box *page 109).*

The sharp pointy end!

Only the bees, social wasps and some ants actually have a sting that they will use in defence. A few of the solitary wasps will use it in hunting and paralysing their prey. All their other relatives use their equivalent egg laying tube for its original purpose for piercing and probing various animals and objects to lay their eggs.

Hymenoptera

The *Hymenoptera*, for that is what scientists call them, consist of the ants, bees, wasps and sawflies. The name refers to their wings. *Hymen* means membrane and *ptera* means wing. One look at a bee or wasp and you can see why – most have two pairs of thin, transparent wings.

Because it is a modified egg laying tube a sting is found only in the females. The sting itself is usually a retractable gadget, that sits in a sheath at the end of the abdomen. It is never used in malice! Bees and wasps have to have a very good reason to get their stings out. Using them is expensive to the insect. If you are a wasp, you will have to make the venom yourself inside a special venom sac: to use this unnecessarily is a waste. If you are a Honey bee the cost is even greater because the sting is barbed like a fishing hook: if it goes into anything but another insect it gets left in its victim and with it comes a bit of the bee. The bee that dealt the blow will usually crawl off and die of its injuries somewhere.

The good bit ...

If all the bees, ants, wasps and sawflies were to vanish from the face of the Earth in the flick of an eye, human society as we know it would start to crumble and pack up. We humans simply cannot live without them! Why?

104

Body design

Rather than run away screaming, watch a bee at a flower – it isn't going to sting you. Look for details and features that give you a clue as to how it lives.

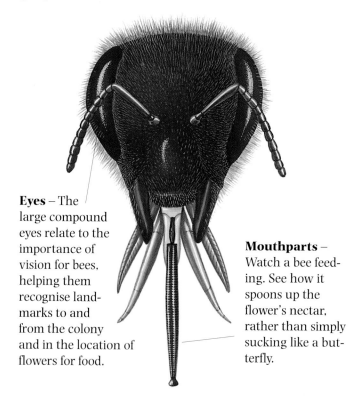

Eyes – The large compound eyes relate to the importance of vision for bees, helping them recognise landmarks to and from the colony and in the location of flowers for food.

Mouthparts – Watch a bee feeding. See how it spoons up the flower's nectar, rather than simply sucking like a butterfly.

Well, we all know that Honey bees make honey, which we find very pleasant. In fact, it was the original sugar and has been used by man for at least 9,000 years. A few thousand years later we had started keeping them and domesticating them in hives. But this is not the reason for their importance; bees and wasps have a major role in pollinating flowers, without which we would have no fruit. In fact, most of the plants we rely on for crops are dependent on pollination.

So much so that many species of bumble bees are employed in greenhouses and introduced to other countries to perform just this task on our behalf.

Life styles of the socialites

The bee that buzzes into mind and is well known in the garden especially in the spring is the bumble bee. That should read bumble bees because there are 19 true species of bumble bee living in Britain and 9 species of look-a-likes, which are parasites. Bumble bees are instantly likeable; they have a rounded cuddly appearance and they often turn up in our gardens well before any other flying insects are around, which makes us notice them even more.

The other common social bee is the Honey bee, *Apis mellifera*. This is a very special insect in many ways. It is thought that it came from somewhere in South-east Asia or Africa and there are drawings on cave walls in China, 9,000 years old, that show humans collecting honey from bee nests. A few thousand years later and we had started to keep them in hives and so started the long history of the domestication of Honey bees.

There are two schools of thought here. Honey bees may have evolved in the tropics but modified their lives just a little in order to deal with colder climates and so spread north into Europe naturally. Or they were introduced here by man as he has spread out around the globe.

The secret to their success is that whether in the Serengeti or Haywards Heath, bees store honey in their combs to see them through the rough times. This can be either the dry season when there are no flowers, or the winter when there are also no flowers! The only difference is the temperature, but bees are naturally very good at maintaining a constant temperature within the nest, by generating more body heat fuelled by this honey store and clustering together as a tight bunch, or cooling down by spreading out, fanning their wings or spreading water around.

Below: *This is one of the most common of the bumble bees,* Bombus hortorum. *Use a field guide for identification. Look at the colour of the bottom and the number and position of stripes for clues.*

Wasp

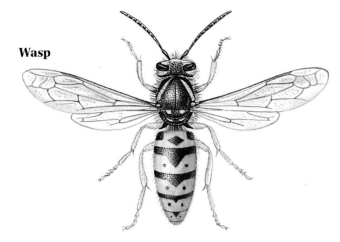

Bee

Wasp (above) or bee (right)? There is no need to fear either. I have seen Honey bees swatted on the basis of misidentification – behaviour that increases your chance of getting

Honey bee or wasp?

Thanks to the popular image of bees as black and yellow stripy things, we tend to grow up with the wrong image in our minds. Because of this I have seen hundreds of young people spot a Honey bee and immediately call it a wasp! The simplest way to tell them apart is that Honey bees are a sort of orangey brown (a similar colour to the runny honey they produce) and quite hairy (see above

Below: *One of the secrets of Honey bee success is their phenomenal ability to communicate with each other, to run an efficient hive and also exploit food sources. Here is the waggle dance of the Honey bee; the angle of the wiggly bit from the vertical coincides with the angle of food source in relation to the sun.*

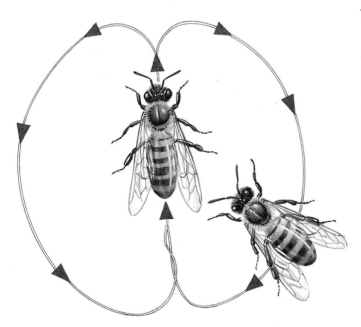

stung! Social wasps have very yellow and black stripes, while honey bees are fluffy with ill-defined stripes of brown and orange.

right). Social wasps are very bold yellow with black bands on their bodies and much funkier in appearance (see above left).

Experiment: Bee school

You may have heard of training dogs, but I bet you did not think you could teach insects! Honey bees communicate with each other and learn to find new flowers rich in pollen and nectar. You can teach the Honey bees in your garden.

You will need:
• *sugar or honey solution*
• *a selection of different coloured cardboard cut outs of flowers (try blue, red, yellow) about 10 cm in diameter*
• *a selection of jam jar lids or bottle tops*

Space out your flowers and on one place the lid. Put some sugar solution in the lid then watch. Soon a bee will find it and after a few hours it should have attracted a crowd. Carefully remove the sugar mix and place it on another coloured flower. Watch what happens. The bees continue to come to the original colour despite there not being any sweet stuff. How are they finding the food? Is it by sight? Are they smelling the sugar? If they simply follow the sugar around regardless of the colour then they are! Are the bees smelling other bees? Place other flowers of the colour they are trained to nearby – what happens now? If bees visit these as much as the one with the reward, they are locating it by colour alone. If they still keep coming to only the flower with the reward then the presence of the other bees or the position of the flower has something to do with it.

Right: *Honey bees and many other insects hum in huge numbers around the few good supplies of pollen and nectar in early spring. Catkins of Pussy willow are one of the best places for them to shop.*

Early starters

Bumble bees have very fat and furry bodies compared with other members of the bee family. They are able to get their nesting and breeding underway a lot quicker in the season because of this and a few other neat adaptations.

The hairy coat keeps the insect warm. By sitting still, disengaging its wings from its flight muscles (taking the wings out of gear), the bee can vibrate these big muscles very quickly. This is like you or I running on the spot, we are not getting anywhere, but we are getting hot. The bumble bee is doing the same and this is warming its body up, either ready for active flight or even to incubate her brood. Like a bird she sits hunched over her eggs, exposing a naked brood patch on the underside of her body. Using this technique, even when there is a late spring frost, turning your lawn silver and nipping your fruit trees in the bud, deep below the surface of the soil there could be a queen bumble bee, snug in her well insulated nest, generating a temperature of 30–32 °C.

Being able to do this means the bumble bee can beat all the other insects to the rewards offered by flowers early in the spring.

Below: Bombus pascuorum.
Not all bumble bees are big, bold and stripy.

Temperature control

Honey bees use a different approach by being absolute masters at nest temperature control. During the winter months Honey bee workers cluster together around their queen in the very centre of their nest. Here, fuelled by the store of honey, they can generate their own heat. By just being alive their bodies create heat. If it gets colder, they cluster tighter together. The temperature in the centre rarely falls below 17 °C and more often than not remaining in the 30 °C range. When the spring days come, they can go out and forage when conditions are good, otherwise they just stay indoors, eat honey and keep on with the chores. They simply keep going year in year out like this, for as long as the queen survives in the nest.

Attracting bees and wasps

You can go about making your garden wasp and bee friendly, firstly by planting lots of nectar and pollen rich flowers, which incidentally are also highly attractive to other insects such as butterflies and moths. Secondly, you can make nest sites and construct desirable residences for your bees and wasps, in the same way you might go about building nest boxes for garden birds (see page 109).

Above: *The old queen performs a spectacular exodus accompanied by a mass of workers. This swarm is looking for a place to start a new hive.*

Bee cycle

Bumble bees have an annual cycle, unlike Honey bee colonies. They start and finish the whole colony life in one year. One of our commonest and most widespread bumble bees, *Bombus terrestris* is also sometimes called the Buff-tailed bumble bee. It starts its lifecycle early on a warm spring day. As soon as the soil has warmed up, the big bundle of furry insect body wakes up. The queen has been deep in a crevice in the soil all winter, for five or six months she has been living off the fat reserves in her body, her battery pack to get her through. Also inside her body she has a store of sperm from her mate last summer. On awakening, she will feed on nectar and pollen from early flowers, then after a while you will notice these bees searching around, investigating any crack, crevice or dark place.

Pollen baskets
The queen selects a suitable nest site, usually an old mouse nest, although it can be pretty much any kind of cavity as long as it is dry and well insulated. She will stock it with a pad of pollen which she collects in special hairs called baskets on her hind legs. She then models waxy secretions from her body to form a rough cell around the pollen pad into which she lays her eggs. At the same time she builds herself a little wax cup, which is provisioned with nectar or honey. When the larvae hatch, she rears them on a mixture of pollen and nectar. Eventually, these then pupate in a cocoon of silk.

When the weather is good, look out for these new queens, they are easy to recognise by size. If you see one collecting pollen (in two large yellow lumps on her hind legs), you know she is provisioning the nest. It is possible to follow these queens back and find out where the nest is.

First generation
Look out also for the first generation of workers in the spring. They are the little bumble bees you will see flying around. The reason they are so small is that they were reared single handedly by the queen on not a lot of food, so they turn out a little stunted and die quite soon.

Once there are enough hatched out to take over the foraging, the queen stops foraging herself and concentrates on egg laying and cell building. The colony swells until a period in the summer when there can be several hundred bees in the nest. During the peak of the colony the queen's influence weakens over the rest and new queens and males are produced, after which the colony structure breaks down slowly. Successfully mated females go into hiding. As soon as they have provisioned themselves and built up their fat reserves, they seek a cool, usually north-facing bank and get their heads down until next spring.

Make a bee bank

This is not so much a construction but a garden feature. To work best it needs to get the sun for a good portion of the day, and so be south facing. In the wild these insects like these hot little sun traps.

Left: Bombus terrestris. *The Buff-tailed bumble bee – another fabulous bumble bee.*

Heap soil up into a bank, make sure it is free draining and away from shade creating plants. If your soil is too moist, mix in some sand and small pebbles. Allow it to settle and keep patches free from vegetation and you should get mining bees and others excavating their burrows.

You can make it more attractive to other bees and wasps by incorporating into the structure a pile of logs stacked up. Drill a selection of different sized holes in these, both in the ends and in their sides. This will also attract those that are particular about wood. For example, there is a colony of bees living in some old nail holes in a telegraph pole down my street!

If you have masonry walls, you can try drilling a few holes in these or even in the mortar between the bricks as this often proves popular with masonry bees.

You could even try placing fence posts, suitably drilled all around your garden, the only limit on what you can try is your interest in these insects and your wallet.

Experiment: The can of straws

This is a neat and simple way of creating a perfect place for solitary bees and wasps. Many species will hole up in

Above: *A bumble bee worker rummages around in a knapweed flower collecting pollen and nectar. These bees are very approachable and are well worth watching.*

the wild in hollow stems and the excavations of other insects, especially those left by wood boring beetles and the like. You can have a go at recreating the conditions for at least some of them by making a bee box. *See panel below.*

Making your bee box

1 Collect old hollow twigs and plant stems of different diameters, such as the dead stems of hogweed, bamboo garden canes, buddleia stems, elder twigs, grasses and reed, and even paper drinking straws.
2 Now fill a container such as an old coffee, plastic flower pot, baked bean tin, or the bottom half of a plastic drinks bottle with these stems. Trim them so they are more or less flush with the rim of the container.
3 Next attach it with string, wire or twine to the stem of a shrub, tree trunk or a garden cane. The advantage of the last is that you can move it around. Two essentials to bear in mind when fixing your nest boxes up is that the entrances should all be sloping down slightly. This stops them getting water logged when it rains. The nests should also be placed in a sunny, open location, preferably south facing – these insects like it hot!

Planet of the Ants

Sadly, we normally react to these top insects in one of two ways: on discovery of a nest close to our homes, we reach, without much thought, for the insecticide or boil a kettle to douse the unfortunate colony! What are we worried about? Do we subconsciously realise what mighty empires they run? Are we a little jealous of their immaculate house keeping? Where there is one ant you just know there are more not far away! The other reaction is that we simply ignore them, spending the rest of our lives just seeing them as little dots scampering around on the ground and never getting our knees dirty, getting down to their level and seeing them for what they are ... cool creatures.

There are around 50 different kinds of ant in the British Isles and if you tried to identify any of them you would probably end up going mad. So we will have a little look at a few of the common ones just to give you a teaser into their lives.

I strongly recommend making a formicarium (see page 114). It may seem like a lot of hassle but it really does open up a window on the lives of these bustling little animals. I hadn't kept ants since I was 11 years old, but for this book I thought I would get a colony going for a bit of inspiration ... wow! I'm an ant addict again!

Above: *These Wood ants are giving this ladybird a hard time; perhaps it was eating their herd of aphids. In the same way a shepherd protects his flock, the ants care for their aphids.*

controls the colony's actions with various smelly chemicals called pheromones.

The colonies consist of the queens' daughters, none of which breed themselves. In this way each nest behaves rather like a single animal. Ants are fine weather insects, not liking the colder climates very much, and compared with the rest of the world we have a very sparse selection of the 9,000 or so species that exist.

What is an ant?

Ants are small wingless wasps and they have been busying themselves on planet Earth for the best part of 80 million years. As well as being survivors they are also one of the most successful groups of animals on the planet today. If the Earth belongs to anything, then it is Planet of the Ants!

They live in the same sorts of colonies as the highly social bees and wasps with a queen or several queens depending on the species. It is the queen who wears the trousers so to speak. She lays all the eggs and she also

Lifecycles

We need to consider the whole colony as a living organism in its own right. You can almost think of the nest as an animal and each ant as a cell. When ants go out on foraging trails they become the eyes and nose and arms of the colony, searching and sniffing out food and other resources to pick up and bring back to the nest.

One of the commonest, most widespread and familiar of the British ants is the common Black pavement ant, *Lasius niger*, (and right on cue just to prove this last statement, one lone worker has just scampered across my desk and over the keyboard of my computer!). This species is probably as good a model as any species for a run down of the life of a colony.

Sexodus

Nature's biggest one night stand happens in mid to late summer. It's this great natural party in the sky that starts the lives of many colonies.

Thousands of black ants erupt from the cracks in patios, tarmac and paving slabs. Hidden beneath the artificial crust humans tend to cover their world in, each colony has been pampering its winged royalty, the males and the potential future queens of new colonies. When the winged sexual generation takes to the air on one sticky August afternoon, it is accompanied by a general turmoil. Ant colonies you have hardly even registered

spill out, a frenzy of workers on security alert for this mass royal wedding. You may not see them, but on some environmental cue – it could be day length, temperature or humidity – every ant nest in the neighbourhood will be engaged in the launch, ensuring that the maximum genetic mixing occurs. They spiral up into the air; they mate on the wing, tree and roof tops.

The queens return to the ground, and get rid of their wings by twisting, rubbing and pulling at them with

Above: *In spring, look under stones to find ant nests. Ants use the stones like storage heaters; the stones warm up in the sun and release this energy slowly to the ants below.*

their jaws. They will never fly again. The males die; their task is complete. The new queen has enough sperm inside her body to last her all of her life. She stores this and uses it when she chooses to control the sex of her offspring.

Right: *Like butterflies and moths, ants have a complete lifecycle. This means they have egg, larval, pupal and adult stages, all of which can be seen at once if you lift a stone with a nest under it. On being disturbed in their colony, workers can be seen to grab anything pale and white and run for cover. Small white grains that look like clusters of dry semolina will be the eggs. Larger elongated, maggot-like objects will be the larvae or grubs. Slightly yellow, large oval objects are cocoons, made of ant silk. Inside (shown here with cocoon removed) are the ant pupae.*

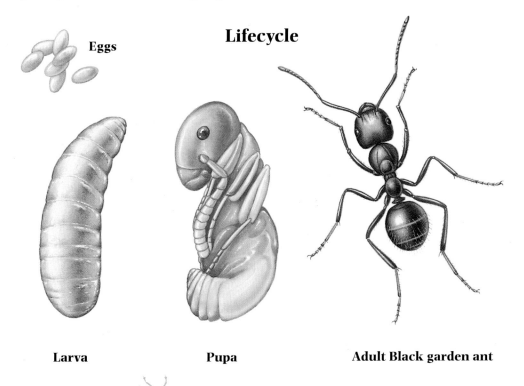

Lifecycle

Eggs

Larva

Pupa

Adult Black garden ant

Left: Every year, usually on a hot, August day, Black pavement ants erupt from their nests. Winged males and future queens engage in a mass winged orgy of mating.

Below: Many birds and other insect-eating animals cash in on the brief superabundance. Fortunately, the ants flood the market and enough succeed in not being eaten for there to be new ant colonies the following year.

Single mum

The new queen on her return to Earth may be adopted by another nest or even the one she just left but more often than not she goes about founding her own empire.

She finds a small hole, crack or cavity in the soil or under a rock and seals herself in. This is known as her claustral cell. She then lays her first eggs and rears the grubs or larvae that hatch from them to be the first workers of the colony. Until they are ready and tottering around she will not emerge into the outside world, not even to feed. She relies on fat reserves in her body and the big wing muscles that powered her first and only flight.

Once she has her first work force, she can sit back and be pampered and fed by her daughters and get down to the serious business of laying eggs for the rest of her life.

Colony rules

The queen lays more and more eggs, and with more and more helpers being produced the colony just gets bigger and bigger, expanding throughout the next year or so.

Lift a stone or peer into your formicarium and you will see just how organised things are. There are chambers containing eggs, larvae of different ages and sizes and of course the pupae.

Nuptial flights

Lots of insect-eating animals cash in on the superabundance of protein when ants undergo their nuptial flights. Look for newly fledged Swallows and House martins, Starlings, sparrows, even Black-headed gulls, all feasting on flying ants.

You will notice that the ants are all busy but if you can follow a few individuals with your eyes, you will notice that they tend to stick to certain jobs. This is an ant's lot. If you emerged from a cocoon in this nest you would carry out a number of different jobs during your life, a kind of job promotion scheme.

You might start as a nurse ant, working on looking after the broods of eggs and larvae, constantly cleaning them, feeding them and moving them around to the part of the nest which has the best humidity and temperature for them to grow up in – full time baby sitters.

Then you may get to work on the nest, building extensions and mending bits as they collapse. One look at an ants' nest tells you there is a lot of this going on all the time, but ants are rather haphazard builders compared to the bees and wasps.

Finally you would be put out to forage for food. You would become a living tea trolley for the rest of the ants, returning to the colony with a crop full of food, which you feed to all those ants that do not get out much.

Once the nest reaches a certain size, the queen allows for the production of more virgin queens and males.

Above: *The hustle and bustle of life in the ant colony can be sampled by lifting a stone. Here you can see workers scurrying off with larvae.*

Above: *Fierce carnivores, ants will hunt down, kill and remove to the nest any animal that cannot defend itself. They will tackle prey much bigger than themselves.*

These are produced in the nest during the summer and here they wait for those muggy, warm conditions for the big mating flights that start the whole thing off.

This continues as long as the queen lives, which can be as long as ten years!

What do ants eat?

Stake out a Wood ants' nest and watch one of the trails leading to it. The ants moving toward the nest will be carrying all manner of items, and the trail of these industrious insects looks like a scaled down conveyor belt of goodies from the Generation Game. The only difference is the items being carried by the ants are invertebrates: worms, flies, caterpillars, aphids, some in pieces, some dead and dying.

This is what the ants are feeding their larvae on, protein rich and packed with goodness, perfect for the developing grubs. Most species are omnivores feeding on a mixture of both meat and plants. Some rely on certain sources more than others, for example some ants feed on protein-rich seeds. But for the most part much of the vegetable bit in their diets comes from honey dew produced by those little bugs, the aphids (see *Ant farmers*).

The aphids benefit from the ants by getting protection from predators and if there were no ants around to clean up the sticky honey dew they would get health problems due to fungus, and disease would start to kill them.

Ants and aphids only get on some of the time. There are aphids which ants do not seem to milk and nobody really knows why this is, as they also produce honey dew! And the relationship between those ants and aphids that do get on can break down from time to

time, especially if conditions become too crowded in the herd or it's getting late in the year. When the time comes the ants perform a culling routine, slaughtering their stock and taking the aphids back to the ever-hungry grubs.

Other sugary supplements that the ants eat include the occasional flower, as these are rich in nectar. Some plants even encourage ants to patrol their leaves and stems by paying them off with a sugary secretion produced by devices called extra-floral nectaries – just look at the base of bracken leaves for these little swollen pits being visited by ants.

Ant farmers

If you watch ants visiting a greenfly colony on your garden plants you will see them stroking the little bugs in a way reminiscent of a person milking a cow. Instead of milk the aphid delivers a little drop of honey dew, which is really plant sap that has passed through the bug's body. The ants go crazy for this stuff as it fuels all the running about they do. Some ants farm these aphids, moving them around to new pastures, and certain ants even build little 'cow sheds' of soil over the bases of the plant stems to keep the aphids safe and protected. This is taken to extremes in the ants that farm the various root aphids. Down in the soil ants are doing much the same thing with aphids that are feeding on the roots of plants. These ants build their own nests around their aphid herds.

Left: *Wood ants make mound nests that look pretty disorganised on the surface but are in fact cleverly constructed to help the ants keep warm in many ways. The vegetation itself generates heat as it rots. The thousands of ant bodies all produce heat too.*

Window into the world of ants – Making your formicarium

Of all the doing bits in the book this is one of the most complicated and it is critical you follow the instructions and get the measurements right otherwise your ants might escape. Making a formicarium or ant city is the best way to get to know ants, as the secret of their society is usually underground, or at least under a stone! It's best to start this in early spring.

You will need:
- *Plaster of Paris*
- *Jug*
- *Jam jar with lid*
- *Spoon*
- *Plywood for base*
- *Strips of wood (approximately 2 cm x 2 cm in cross section): 1 x 30 cm, 2x 20 cm and 3 x 12 cm*
- *Modelling clay*
- *Clear rubber pipe (at least 30 cm long)*
- *Sheet of hard, clear plastic*
- *Black cloth or paper*
- *Ants with soil*
- *duck tape*
- *wood glue*
See panel below.

Making your formicarium

For a more thorough explanation, see page 115.

1 Make the frame.
2 Make a system of tunnels and chambers.
3 Mix up the plaster of Paris and pour into the mold.
4 Fill the cavities with soil.
5 Add your ants.

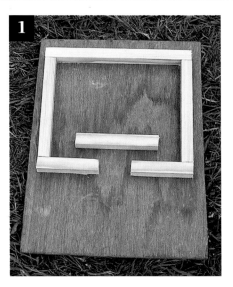

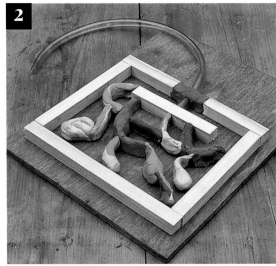

1 To make the formicarium you need to glue the frame of wood strips to the base as in the diagram. With the three 12 cm long pieces, make a staggered wall with a gap in the centre, this will be the entrance. Just beyond this gently place the remaining 12 cm strip of wood. This need not be glued down as it will be removed because it is just part of the mould.

2 Next, using the modelling clay, make a system of tunnels and chambers, remember these have to be as deep as the frame. What is now modelling clay will eventually be the living space and corridors for your ants. Remember to completely fill the entrance with the clay and ensure the modelling clay tunnels butt up to the loose 12 cm wooden strip. Place the lid of hard clear plastic on top at this stage; it helps you to see whether the modelling clay is high enough. If you have got the height right the clay should squish gently against the plastic.

3 Leave a plug of modelling clay in the entrance, and push one end of the clear plastic tube through it. The end of the tube in the nest should also butt up tightly to the loose piece of 12 cm wood as in the diagram. This makes a high street out of the nest.

4 Mix up the plaster of Paris in the jug into a runny solution and pour it into the gaps until it comes to the top of the frame and fills all the space not taken up by the modelling clay and piece of wood. Allow the plaster of Paris to set for a day or so. Then pull out the modelling clay and 12 cm piece of loose wood. What you will be left with is a series of tunnels in the plaster of Paris.

5 Fill the cavities left by the modelling clay with well drained soil. Attach a jam jar to the end of the entrance tube outside of the nest. Allow the tube to enter the jar through a hole made in the lid. The tube must be flush with the inside of the lid, and you should seal any gaps with more modelling clay. Place the hard, clear plastic lid on the nest and secure and make completely ant proof with duck tape.

6 Collect some ants. The Black pavement ants are best, although Red ants can be used as well. Look for their nests under stones, tin and wood. They are best collected in early spring as they cluster together and can easily be scooped up in their entirety. For your colony to thrive you need to be guaranteed a queen and a good selection of workers, eggs and pupae.

7 Introduce them into the jam jar and add a little cotton wool and soak it in weak sugar solution. Then cover your newly made formicarium with the black card or cloth leaving the jam jar exposed to the light. This gives your ants a nice dark atmosphere to set up their new ant city and will encourage them to leave the jar for the formicarium.

Right: *The Yellow lawn ant occurs commonly in ... lawns! These pale yellow ants live underground most of the time, so you will see them only if you dig up or disturb your lawn.*

To start with the ants will seem in complete turmoil but soon they will organise themselves and start to move into the formicarium. Leave them in the dark for a few days and let them become established. You can now add different food types in the jam jar. They require sugar, water and protein, which you can provide with honey, damp cotton wool, insects (collect these from window sills – alive and dead – the ants will use them) and seeds.

Assuming you got a healthy queen when you collected the ants, you will soon notice the numbers start to increase as the workers rear more recruits and the queen lays more eggs. Make sure you keep the whole formicarium in a warm location but out of the way of direct sunlight and provide the ants with plenty of food and water – you can simply substitute the jam jar with a new one, when you need to clean it out.

Look after these basic needs and treat them with respect and the ants will give up many of their secrets. Every day you will notice something different. Enjoy observing them – you will not fail to be amazed.

Ant armoury

Have you ever been kneeling or lying in the grass relaxing in the sun and suddenly your skin feels like it's on fire? You have just experienced the phenomenon known as 'Ants in the pants!' These ants belong to the group known as the *Myrmicine* ants and include a number of the red ants that you might come across in the garden.

The reason they hurt so much is that each worker disturbed by your blunderings has taken you as a threat to the nest and sunk its sting into you. It is the sting and its venom which hurt so much, a defensive gadget just like the hypodermic weapon of the wasps and bees.

The other kinds of ant are the *Formicine* ants. These include the Black and Wood ants. They do not have a sting. They bite with their large, strong mandibles and this, combined with the enthusiastic squirting of formic acid from a pore at the tip of their abdomen (all that is left of the sting), ensures that those attacked do not forget the meeting in a hurry. A colony of Wood ants can produce so much of this effective chemical deterrent that if

you placed a short candle on the nest and lit it, the ants would eventually put it out.

Despite the ants' tendency to become quick-fire living acid cannons at the slightest provocation, some birds will actually welcome their attentions. Jays and woodpeckers will quite happily sit and spread themselves out on these nests. It is thought that the acid from the ants rids them of parasites that live in their feathers.

Left: *Red ant.*
Below: *Ants will be quick on the draw, squirting anything strange or threatening in, on or near the nest with a jet of formic acid. This can be enough to extinguish a naked flame.*

Recruitment and communication – Pass the parcel and chemical bread trail

Another reason for the success of ants is their efficient communication system. They use scent in a very clever way. Have you ever looked down and seen the odd ant randomly walking about on the patio?

She and probably several hundred other ants just like her are all doing pretty much the same all over the place. One of the advantages to ants is their size, or lack of it. Ants are famously small. Not only do they not attract too much attention but they also can get places. For every one ant on the patio, there'll be another on the wall, a few in the borders, a couple around the dustbin, several on the lawn and so on. Some species get into our kitchens through the tiniest crack.

But to think that such a small creature cannot make much odds would be a mistake. All it takes is for one to get lucky and find a pile of desirable food and the secret of why ants are so successful will slowly unfurl. Next time you are on the patio and you see an ant, place a dollop of jam in front of it and sit back and watch. You feel like a camera cop on a police documentary – from your position you can see the action.

What you cannot detect is the world of smell and micro smell that the ant lives in. To start with the ant will probably fill both of its stomachs, the first one is a crop and this contains the food that is often shared around the colony, a kind of community stomach.

But despite the two stomachs, the ant is still carrying only a little food and the jam represents a mountain of useful resources which the individual has not even made a dent into yet.

It will then run back to the nest, dragging its abdomen along the ground. It is leaving a chemical bread trail a track of perfume that is dribbled from glands such as the Dufours gland in the ant's abdomen. This will not last forever and will start to evaporate quickly. Back at the nest, other workers are met, greeted with lots of excited antennae waving and they will set off along the trail, smelling the vapour as it wafts up from the ground. Soon this is repeated by lots of ants, each reinforcing the scent trail and this is why it is not uncommon to find hundreds of them clustered around a particularly useful substance. Your blob of jam may well

Dust the trail

Wet your finger and stick it in some dusting talcum powder. It sticks. A way of demonstrating the ants' scent trail is to use this principle. Try to persuade an ant returning to the nest to walk over a piece of glass or Perspex. Then as soon as it has, sprinkle some talc on the glass and blow the excess off. What you might just be able to see, is a faint line of talc where it has stuck to the liquid the ant has oozed out of its bottom! This is a neat trick but it doesn't work very well with all species and some ants leave better trails. Give it a go!

be in great demand back at the nest and if you stay long enough or even revisit every few minutes, you will notice just how effective their numbers are. As the food is used up and taken back to the nest, the number of workers returning decreases, the concentration of the scent trail peters out and no more ants return.

A particularly frantic recruitment drive will often result in a bit of an ant motorway backwards and forwards from the nest. You can once again demonstrate the presence of an invisible trail by wiping your finger through the line. Watch what happens as the ants are thrown into confusion until one accidentally stumbles upon it and picks it up again.

Below: *Ants use trails of smell to follow their leader to food or find their way back to the nest. You can see how dependent they are on this by gently wiping the ground through a trail with your finger.*

Bugs – A Shed Load of Suckers!

Just flick open the bug section in a good field guide and what you see before you is an amazing array of beasts – furry ones, funky coloured ones, some suck sap, others suck blood, a few walk on water, some crawl, some hop, lots fly and swim. There are over 1,600 different species in Britain and Ireland! Believe me there is stuff happening out there you would not believe.

Body design

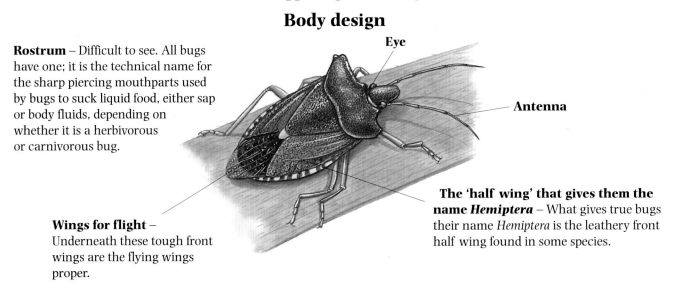

Rostrum – Difficult to see. All bugs have one; it is the technical name for the sharp piercing mouthparts used by bugs to suck liquid food, either sap or body fluids, depending on whether it is a herbivorous or carnivorous bug.

Eye

Antenna

The 'half wing' that gives them the name *Hemiptera* – What gives true bugs their name *Hemiptera* is the leathery front half wing found in some species.

Wings for flight – Underneath these tough front wings are the flying wings proper.

Escape tactics

Despite looking completely defenceless, aphids have a number of escape tactics. Tickle a colony with a paint brush. You will see a lot of the aphids simply let go of the twig or bud on which they were feeding. Some will also present their rear end to an attacker and ooze a waxy substance out of the two prongs – called siphunculi – either side of their abdomen. This is sticky and unpleasant especially as it solidifies on the mouthparts or the eyes of a ladybird. The odour of the wax acts as an alarm call to other aphids which simply unplug their mouthparts from the plant and walk or drop off.

What is a bug?

The technical name for the family is *Hemiptera*, which means half wing, and this refers to the distinctive half leathery and half delicate wings of some species. The one tool that all bugs have and which distinguishes them from beetles and all other insects is their sharp needle-like mouthparts.

All the true bugs, from herds of greenfly, to pretty shield bugs and pond skaters, use those sharp mouthparts but for very different jobs. Some use them like a straw, plugging into succulent plants for their juice; others use them like a dagger, for stabbing prey or even in defence.

It's a bug's lifecycle!

Bugs grow up without a pupal stage. On hatching from the eggs they look just like their parents, just smaller and without wings. Then they proceed to get on with eating. They grow, as do all insects, by a series of skin splitting episodes, usually four, until they reach adulthood.

But in the wacky world of the aphid (those humble, soft-bodied micro-bugs that do such a good job of ruining the summer of many a gardener) they go a step further. Let's just take the common Blackfly as an example.

It sits out the unproductive winter months as an egg, secreted away in a crack of the bark of a secondary host plant such as the Spindle tree or Guelder rose.

As the spring warms up, the eggs hatch and the young nymphs plug into the unfurling sap-rich shoots. Four moults later they have quickly grown into plump little females, all of which begin to produce clones of themselves. This continues until clusters of blackfly adorn the shoots and buds. The speed they breed at is accelerated as the temperatures rise.

Then there comes a trigger – probably overcrowding. If they were to stay, the plant would be drained and they would eventually damage the host and run out of sap. So rather than go hungry, a generation is

Above: *Use a beating tray to look for bugs (see page 71).*

born as flying machines. These have changed their tastes. The winged individuals fly off to find a new summer host in other plants such as docks, thistles and beans.

Below: *Mother bug. Not all species show the same degree of tenderness toward their newly hatched young as this Parent bug. She is so named for her mothering of the eggs and young nymphs, which she guards from predator and parasite.*

Bug lifecycle

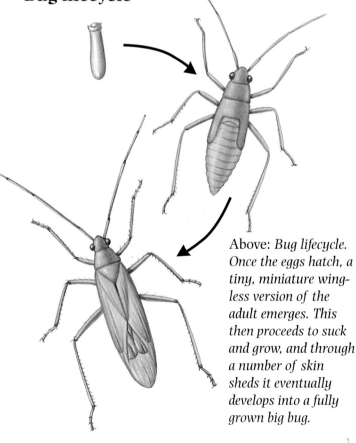

Above: *Bug lifecycle. Once the eggs hatch, a tiny, miniature wingless version of the adult emerges. This then proceeds to suck and grow, and through a number of skin sheds it eventually develops into a fully grown big bug.*

Left: *Bubble bum. Cuckoo spit is nothing to do with the bad habits of that early spring bird, but a defence whipped up by a young Froghopper. Part the bubbles gently and you will see the maker! This one is an adult Froghopper.*

They then settle down and go about the business of breeding and feeding all over again, until the days shorten. Then a generation of winged females is born. They fly back to the winter host plants and give birth to a generation of egg-laying females. Back on the summer host plants, the shrinking numbers here give rise to winged males. These then fly off and seek out the egg laying females in the few hours that they have to live as adults. After mating the females lay tiny eggs in the bark ready once more to see out the winter. Phew! That's one long and complicated lifecycle!

Greenfly on a stick!

Anyone who has tried to grow plants will have encountered the incredible potential of aphid populations to expand. Take a stem with only a few Greenfly or Blackfly on and place it in a vase indoors. Select a stem without any winged animals; you do not want to introduce these guys to your house plants.

Keep an eye on the big ones; these will be the adult females and assuming you are in the middle of summer, they will be in full swing. As well as excreting globules of plant sap called honey dew from their behinds, they pop out the occasional baby aphid! This is virgin birth – no male required, no time wasted with courtship. They just churn out lots of little replicas or clones.

This is a rare enough occurrence anywhere in nature, but aphids are rather good at it. Some species can turn out up to ten young a day like this. Each of these mothers is not just giving birth to daughters, but inside these daughters are fully developed embryos of their granddaughters too. If all of these survive, the single female can give rise to over 6 million aphids in two months!

A bug for every occasion
There are so many different species, in so many different shapes and sizes that there is no way I can show them all here. However, there are a few that you will bump into in the exploration of the microcosm that is in your back garden or park.

Experiment: Bubble bum

Every spring little gobs of foaming spit appear, seemingly splattered around in our gardens and hedgerows. What is this stuff? Well, it certainly isn't produced by a cuckoo with bad habits! Cuckoo spit is actually the clever invention of the young stages of the common green Froghopper.

The bubbles are a kind of DIY camouflage, to protect the young nymph from being knobbled by pretty much any animal that likes eating small vulnerable bugs! Take a fine camel hair artist's paintbrush and a pot of water. Gently dab at the bubbles, wiping them off with the wet brush until the little green insect is revealed. It will probably be aware its cover has been blown, and will hide on the other side of the plant stem. If you leave it now, it will plug its sharp straw-like mouthparts back into the stem and before your very eyes you can watch it blow a new cover from its bottom. The bubble liquid is actually the plant sap that has passed right through the insect.

Later on in the spring you may stumble upon froth of a slightly different consistency. This is the cocoon from which the nymph makes its final moult into a winged adult. Do not wait for them to make a new bubble screen, because they can't. It is a skill that only the nymphs use.

Shield bugs

There are over 40 different kinds of these, some of the most spectacular and largest of the land loving bugs. Most are flat and quite a few are shield-shaped.

The other name for them is stink bugs – pick one up and smell your fingers afterwards. You have just been bugged! They ooze a very smelly distasteful chemical from glands in their thorax.

Some advertise themselves with bright colours as a way of warning any animal stupid or tasteless enough to try eating one.

Bugs on film – Pond skaters,
Water measurers and Water crickets

Fishing is a perfect way of passing the day, and entomologists have their own version of this hobby. I call it tweaking for bugs. Watching these chaps walk on water and cast their little spangled star shadows on the bottom of a pond or river is one of the joys of being a bug person in summer.

The quarry are those unusual bugs that live a life of limbo, straddling, in more ways than one, the fragile film between the air and the water. There are many species but they fall into three main categories: pond skaters, which hop and slide quickly on the surface of still or slow-moving water, of which there are eight species in Britain; water crickets, not crickets at all but a shorter, bent-legged version of the above; and the slow and lazy water measurers.

All these insects are bugs in the true sense of the word and all are carnivorous, using their sharp stylets to pierce the bodies of their prey and suck the juices out.

They use the surface film for many things: they can use vibration to set up ripples to communicate with each other. Other insects drown because they don't have all the adaptations of the water bugs. In their struggles, they make ripples. These attract the attentions of our bugs, which detect the little waves with their feet. The bugs home in on these and speed up the death of the unfortunate insect. You can

Above: *Hawthorn shield bug. The shield bugs are a group, that look a little bit like – you guessed it – shields! This one is sitting on some berries.*

see just how effective this is by taking a piece of thin cotton or fine fishing line. Scavenge around in windows for a fresh fly corpse, carefully tie this to one end of the line and then tie the other to a garden cane or stick. Gently

Below: *The Water measurer's slow lazy pace is unlikely for a predator, but this pond surface bug does not have to move fast to catch dinner; usually it is held firmly by the surface tension of the water.*

Above: *The Black aphid in its aeronaut get up. These garden pests go through different stages in their lifecycle; the winged individuals help to spread the populations around.*

wiggle and giggle the stick so that your fly puts out ripples. Keep an eye on the nearest Pond skater or Water bug. As soon as it gets the message of ripples away it rows, scooting towards its meal.

If you now gently pull the fly and its now firmly attached scavenger close to the bank, you can watch at your leisure the grizzly act as the bug uses its long stylets to probe, pierce and suck out the juices.

Below: *Quick to colonise new areas of water, many bugs, like this Water boatman or Backswimmer, live below the surface where most terrorise small pond residents with their carnivorous habits.*

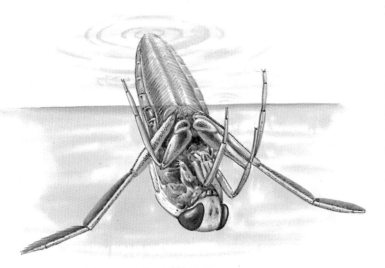

Aphids – herds of little suckers

These are probably the most successful of the bugs. They have closely shadowed the development of plants for 280 million years. Of the 500 different kinds found in the UK most species are very specialised, only having one or two hosts. Few of these are actually pests, but those that are make up for their lack of number by being very good at being pests.

Many simply live a quiet life underground on plant roots. Aphids are sap suckers, it is what they do. They drink huge quantities of the sugar-rich liquid found in plants. The problem is they need protein to grow like they do, and plant sap doesn't have much protein, so to get their daily recommended dose they drink loads of it.

Lots of liquid in, means lots of liquid out – this is the sugary, sticky liquid called honey dew. It's what drives ants crazy and it's what drives car owners who park underneath lime and sycamore trees in the summer crazy too!

Water bugs

The water bugs are a motley bunch and not all of them can actually swim very well, which comes as a bit of a surprise. Densely weeded pools are what these creatures like. One of the highlights of any pond dipping session is to peer into a weed-filled net and notice one of the plant stems get up and start walking off. This is the Water stick-insect – a bad name and a good name all in one. Yes, it looks like a stick insect, but it isn't even closely related to one! It is yet another peculiar bug. Big eyes, stout beak and big raptorial front legs a bit like a Praying mantis, just waiting to stretch out and give a death hug to any passing small fish, tadpole or insect, make this one a shady character. The big pointy thing sticking out of its back end is not a sting as is often claimed, but no more than a snorkel, which draws air from the surface, and stores it under the wings, where it is absorbed by the spiracles on the abdomen.

Courtship sounds

The Lesser water boatman is one of the few pond insects to use sound in its courtship. If you keep a few of these insects in a tank for observation, just keep your ears open for a squeaky, rasping song, particularly noticeable during the quiet times of the day of evening and morning. This sound is produced by the male, which rubs his bristly front legs on a ridge on the side of his head.

A similar but stouter looking beast is the equally badly named Water scorpion. This animal has all the above features but in a more compact style.

The other more active species include the frisbee flattened Saucer bug, the Backswimmer and the Lesser water boatman. Peer into any water body bigger than a puddle during the summer and you will more often then not see one of these rowing away to the bottom. These are bubble breathing bugs. They trap a layer of air from the surface on their bodies usually between their wing cases and their abdomens and on hairs on the underside of their bodies too.

This portable air supply, which takes on a silvery appearance if you look at one in a jam jar or tank full of water, allows the insects great freedom under water. They are some of the fastest aquanauts in the pond. The Backswimmer and the Saucer bug are both voracious predators, using their mouthparts like a dagger, stabbing and eating anything that is small enough for them to manage.

The Lesser water boatman, which swims the right way up, is the only vegetarian among those mentioned. It uses its rostrum like a vacuum cleaner, sucking up algae and plant debris that it has sorted out with its front legs.

Buggles – the aeronauts

If you make a new pond in your garden or see a bundle of water bugs happily rowing around in a cattle trough, have you ever wondered how they get there? There is a very simple solution to this conundrum.

To solve it, you need to catch an adult insect using a pond net. A big Water boatman is ideal. Because they are big you can see things a lot easier and they are easy to identify as an adult – they are the ones with the silvery white back, which is easy to see when they are flipping around in your net.

Gently remove the insect from the net (try not to squeeze it, lifting is better) as Water boatmen can deliver a painful bite. Hold it in the flat palm of your hand; it may leap about a bit at first, but it isn't in pain, or suffocating. Eventually it will settle down the right way up for you to see, with its back facing up. Now is the time to watch carefully. In my experience the

Above: *Poke around in pond weed and you could well uncover a Water scorpion (though it is not a scorpion at all, otherwise it wouldn't be in this bug chapter, would it?). These two are mating.*

next bit usually happens in a couple of minutes, but it may take longer, depending on a number of things like how sunny it is or the air temperature.

Watch for it to pop the top of its back open like the bonnet of a car and start pumping its abdomen back and forth. This is the sign. The animal will unfold a set of wings and buzz off to find a new pond. Most adult bugs have leathery wings and are extremely good fliers. For pond bugs this is handy as they can check out new homes, or simply make the most of temporary ones!

Below: *Watch one of these shifty guys stalking around in the undergrowth, stabbing unsuspecting insects with that needle sharp beak and you will see how the Assassin bug is such a fierce predator.*

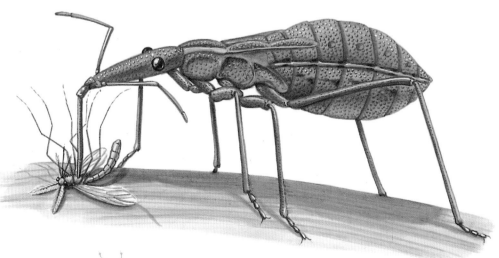

The Beetles – Too Many Species, Too Little Time

You cannot deny the basic beetle is a design classic. With more beetles in the world than any other kind of animal, that's over 350,000 named so far, which makes up over a quarter of all animals on the planet, the proof of their world domination is obvious. What makes beetles so successful? Well, just look at a beetle, its neatest feature is that it is so basic, with a design that nature came up with over 230 million years ago!

Perfect cover

One of the secrets to their huge success is in the wing cases that most beetles have on their back. These highly modified forewings, called elytra, act as perfect covers for the delicately folded rear flying wings.

Some beetles have lost the ability to fly and their elytra have become fused together – handy for the beetle as these provide a nice shiny coat of armour, excellent protection from predators and the environment.

To see for yourself how the elytra and the wings are used in flight, next time you are in the garden just persuade a ladybird or a Chafer beetle to climb onto your hand. When it has crawled to the highest place and sits poised on your fingertip, it usually means it is thinking about flight. The elytra spring open and after a pause the transparent hindwings are carefully unfolded on their delicate micro-hinges, briefly stretched and the beetle goes humming off into the heavens.

Beetles may not be the most graceful of aeronauts, but they still have all the advantages that a life with wings offers.

As well as the wing thing, beetles have simple mouthparts, which means these and the rest of their body can be customised. Go out there in the garden and give a bush a good tap. I bet the majority of animals that fall out of it are beetles. In fact, you could turn upside down any habitat except for those in the polar regions and you would find lots of beetles.

Above: *The biggest insect in Europe, the Stag beetle is not so common as it used to be, probably a victim of our tidy habits, clearing up dead wood on which its grubs live.*

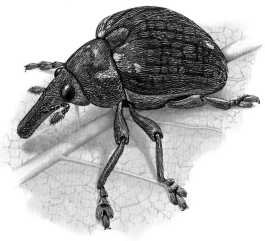

Below: *Aw, come on! It's cute. Weevils are well worth a squint through a hand lens. Despite seeming insignificant to the naked eye, up close they are oozing with as much charisma as a beetle can ooze!*

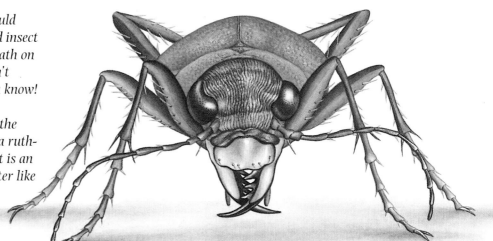

Right: This is the last thing you would want to see if you were a soft-bodied insect that just stepped out onto a sunny path on a summer's day. The Tiger beetle isn't called a Tiger beetle for nothing, you know!

Below right: Not a cute little baby, the young Tiger beetle larva is as much a ruthless killer as its mum and dad. But it is an ambush specialist not an active hunter like its parents.

Demons in the dust

One of those blisteringly hot June days are the best times to go stalking tigers, Tiger beetles that is.

Your first awareness of them is usually their shadow skittering quickly over the sun-baked ground. Their good vision, thermally charged bodies and long legs mean they remain three steps ahead of you all the time, hot footing it. If you get too close they leap into the air spreading their metallic green wing cases and buzzing to safety. Watching them hunting the sandy wastes of heath, dune and moor is best achieved with a pair of close-focusing binoculars but if you team up with a friend you can drive the beetles along a path toward you. If you wait while lying on your belly, you may just get to stare one of these grass root terrorists between the eyes.

To really appreciate their metallic finery and evil-looking mandibles at close quarters, you need to catch a Tiger beetle and view it in a clear plastic pot. Butterfly nets, quickly popped on top of them is in my experience the best way of catching them.

If your morbid curiosity still isn't satisfied, look for small, neat holes about 5 mm in diameter in sun-baked mud or sand at the edge of paths. Using a mirror or a torch illuminate the darkness within and you may find staring back at you one of the strangest creatures you are ever likely to view through a magnifying glass. It is ugly, has a serious appetite and a pair of jaws to match its parents, though it doesn't bother to chase its prey down like a Cheetah. Instead it waits in ambush. With its all around vision, it truly has eyes, not only in the back of its head but at the sides and in front too. In fact, it is safe to say that the Tiger beetle's larvae won't miss a trick.

You can gently exhume these bizarre little grubs by carefully excavating their burrow with a blunt knife or spoon, but when you have finished looking pop it back into a similar sized hole made with a cocktail stick or skewer and the insect will do the rest.

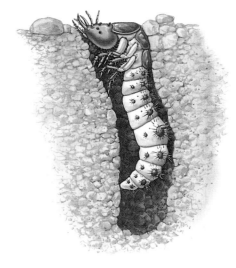

Little ladies

You may know nothing about beetles, but I bet you know what a ladybird looks like and would recognise one instantly. I also suspect that you would also know they are good for the garden because they chomp pest aphids. That's a good start.

But ladybirds start their career in pest control even before they take on their familiar uniform as an adult beetle. You can find these baby ladies fairly easily.

In June or July scour the garden for a plant that is having a hard time of it with aphids; stinging nettles and thistles always seem to have a good population. Look closer still and you will almost certainly find a strange beast. It looks a bit like a caterpillar, grey for the most part but with yellow/orange spots and bristly warts, with a long segmented body. Give it a tickle and the thing goes sprinting off, not in caterpillar style but propelled by six long spindly legs. This is a ladybird, not looking like the ladybird we are familiar with. All beetles go through a lifecycle that has egg, larva, pupa and adult. What you have just found is the larva.

Experiment: Rearing them

Ladybirds are very easy to rear in plastic petri dishes or any clear plastic box, lined with a piece of kitchen towel to absorb any excess moisture.

You will need:
- *clear plastic box*
- *kitchen towel*
- *ladybird larva*
- *aphids*
- *leaves*

Keep no more than ten in each box and try to match them in size. The reason for this is that ladybirds are topnotch predators and although they normally focus their attentions on aphids, if they run short of these or are overcrowded, they will turn cannibalistic.

Make sure that you clean them out every day and place fresh aphids in their pots on leaves and you should

Above: *Aphid masher. This unlikely looking creature acts like a caterpillar, but runs around like it is always late. It is in fact the larva of a seven-spot ladybird.*

get on just fine. In close confinement you will be able to watch as these voracious larvae gobble up hundreds of aphids. If anyone in your family is a gardener they will probably be very interested to look too as this little baby beetle makes mincemeat of the arch enemy.

Look out for skin changes as they grow, there are usually four of these. Just before the larva moults into the pupa, it stops moving, attaches the tip of its abdomen to a surface and hunches up. Do not panic, this is normal behaviour. It is called a pre-pupa and 24 hours later it will have moulted for the last time.

The pupa is a strange mobile thing, which will stand up and down several times if it is touched. It is usually the same colour as the larva, but is still not looking much like a ladybird. Then some two weeks later a plain-looking beetle will crawl out. It will rest for a while, allowing its wing cases to harden and within a couple of days, colours will come to its wing cases and it will finally turn into the kind of insect we know and love – a ladybird.

Below: *This ladybird is emerging from its pupa and is soft and as yet hasn't developed spots. It would be quite a rare sight in the wild, but in captivity you can rear ladybirds in a margarine tub.*

Below: *35 spots! A cluster of five Seven-spot ladybirds, one of the most frequently encountered species. Ladybirds can be red or yellow. Other species include the Ten-spot ladybird and even the Twenty-two-spot ladybird!*

Falling for it – catching beetles out and about

As night falls the big beetles emerge from their lairs and go on the prowl. These are the top predators of the insect underworld ready to run down some unfortunate invertebrate and tear it limb from limb. To a slug the ground beetles are every bit as formidable as a Lion would be to a Gazelle.

You can find some of them by looking for their hidey holes by day, turning over logs, stones and debris. The lazy beetle hunter's technique is a device called a pitfall trap. The principle is a pit – any old canister with deep, smooth slippery sides will do the idea being that you sink this into the ground, the beetle falls in and cannot crawl out.

Experiment: Making your pitfall trap

The most basic design is a tin or jam jar sunk into the ground, with a few dry leaves in the bottom and a stone or tile placed over the top, balanced on a few smaller sticks or stones. You can place these anywhere in the garden and hope that a beetle falls in. This works well enough, but the best trap is a little more sophisticated. *You will need:*

- *Three sticks*
- *String*
- *2 plastic drinks bottles*
- *Skewer*
- *Leaves and twigs*
- *Trowel*
- *Bananas*

  See panel below.

1 Take a large drinks bottle and cut the neck off it with the scissors. This is going to be the pit. One of the problems of these is that they can fill up with rain water and drown the beetles, so using the skewer, make plenty of drainage holes in the bottom of it.

2 Dig a hole deep enough to sink the pit, place the trap in the ground so that the lip is level with that of the soil around it.

3 Take a smaller drinks bottle. With the skewer make a number of holes in the sides and top, in the top two thirds of the bottle and not the bottom part.

4 I have found, and many other professional beetle hunters will back me up on this, that bananas are one of the best baits, especially nice squishy, smelly fermenting ones. So preparation of this a day or so before you go trapping is a good idea. Before you ask, I have no idea why carnivorous beetles are attracted to the smell of rotten fruit, especially one they would never ever come across in the British countryside! Squeeze the bananas a piece at a time into the top of the second bottle, add a bit of sugar, even some yeast and leave in a warm place for a few hours.

5 Back at the trap site, make a wigwam out of sticks and tie them together at the top. Place this over the trap. These must be high enough to allow you to suspend the small bottle with the smelly bait in it over the top of the trap, without touching the ground. Put some dead leaves, twigs and bark in the bottom of the trap, but not so much that any insects can stroll up them like a ladder

Making your pitfall trap

1 The basic design – a pot sunk in the ground is the trap, the tile and stones allow beetles in but stop it filling with rain. Add drainage holes in the bottom. The flag will help you find your trap again the next day.

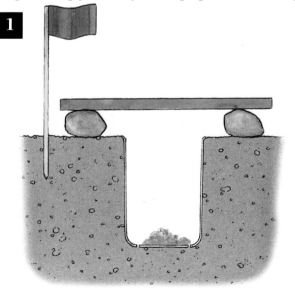

2 The beetle's knees – a deluxe pitfall trap, worth that little bit of extra work. Don't forget the bananas!

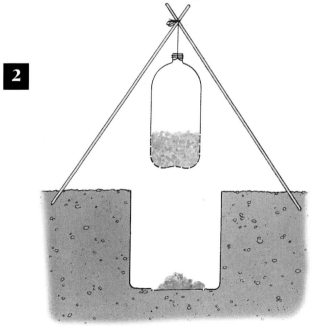

and get out. The idea is that they will fall in then hide themselves away from view of predators and be safe until you find them.

6 It is just a matter of waiting until the morning to see what you get. The more traps you make the more beetles you will catch and the more you will learn about what prowls around your garden. Check the traps at least daily and always first thing in the morning as some of these beetles are so mean that if they are left in the traps for too long they may well start to snack on any of their smaller trap mates.

Beetles about

As you are probably gathering, there are enough interesting beetles to fill a hundred books like this. I am, however, going to have to limit myself to a few of my favourites.

Devil's coach-horse beetle

The Devil's coach-horse beetle has always attracted attention and its name tells us a bit about its history. It was once thought that when it raises its tail in alarm it is casting a spell or curse of the devil on you! What's really happening is that you have scared the living daylights out of this normally secretive animal. The ace it plays is to look as scary as possible, threatening us with a mean pair of jaws held wide open and a tail bent up above its head. The full tail bit of the display is often wasted on us but one of its functions is to emit an unpleasant chemical from organs on the tip.

The animal is not entirely harmless. If you pick it up with bare hands it will give you a nip with those jaws.

The Devil's coach-horse beetle belongs to a family of long wheel base beetles called the *Staphylinids* or rove beetles. They have a long flexible body to allow them to chase their prey into small holes and crevices, hence most are found in the leaf litter. They do still have wings and most can use them to fly. Look for the tiny reduced wing cases.

Above: *The Devil's coach-horse beetle is one of the biggest and due to its habit of raising its abdomen above its head is often mistaken for a scorpion.*

Maybugs

Fizzzzzzzzzzzzzz clunk! is the noise that heralds the arrival of one of these stunning beetles at your window pane. From May onwards these charismatic beetles will often be attracted to lights and are a common catch in a moth trap during the summer months. Maybugs or Cockchafers, with their orange-brown elytra and general fuzziness, are pretty beetles that spend their long adult life of a couple of months munching on plant leaves and breeding. You can sex these beetles by counting the

Below: *Another favourite, the Great diving beetle is truly one of the most spectacular insects you could ever hope to find flipping around in the bottom of your pond net. The equally aggressive larva (below left) is also a good catch.*

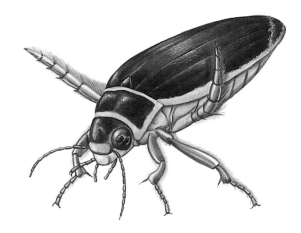

number of veins in their fan-like antennae; males have seven, females six! The larvae are white C-shaped grubs that feed on grass roots for three years. These are eaten by birds such as rooks, hence their other name of rook worms.

Soldiers and sailors

The Soldier and Sailor beetles are easily recognised by being boldly bedecked with reds, oranges and navy-greys. There are four common species: *Cantharis rustica* has blue-grey wing cases and a spot on the pronotum (plate that sits over the thorax); *C. fusca* is similar but with black legs; *C. livida* has brown wing cases; and what I used to refer to as a blood sucker as a kid, *Rhagonycha fulva*, which is redder than the rest with orange wing cases with a black band towards their ends.

Stars in the grass

The sight of a Glow worm often conjures up an image of balmy summer evenings. But how many of us see one and feel sorry for slugs and snails? Find a glowing female and what you are looking at is a murderess.

She's off her food now (she doesn't eat as an adult beetle) but for the last two summers (20 months) as a larvae she will have stabbed, poisoned and consumed many molluscs.

Find the females (look on unimproved grassland on chalky soils) and then search under stones and logs – the sort of habitat in which you might expect to find their prey – for the equally interesting larvae. They look a little like a flattened millipede, black with a pale corner to the rear of each segmented plate and no more than a centimetre long.

If you find an adult female glowing away in the grass, look at her with a torch. I know this spoils the spectacle but you will be able to see how un-beetle like she is and also check the surroundings for any males that have been lured in. These look a bit more like the classic beetle, with wings, elytra and a pair of huge eyes, ideal for spotting the females' light show in the grass below.

Right: If you look at a Glow worm in daylight, you will see the light-producing parts of her body are a pale colour. These are crystals in her body, which when she is glowing, act as mirrors, reflecting her light outwards for all to see. This pair are mating.

Above: *Scour a thistle flower in summer and you will probably see these reddish orange beetles. They are called Soldier beetles and are predators on other small insects that visit the flower.*

Glowing in the dark

The glow of a Glow worm is caused by a chemical reaction, so unlike a light bulb Glow worms do not overheat. The two chemicals that the insect mixes are luciferin and luciferase, which produce a greenish light. The insect can somehow control this and turn on or off certain panes depending on what she is doing.

True Flies and their Look-alikes

We all know what a fly is, don't we? But do we know what a fly isn't? There are several groups of unrelated insects buzzing around that for various reasons tend to get a little bit confused with flies. It doesn't help when a lot of them have the word fly tacked onto the ends of their names despite not being true flies at all, such as dragonfly, mayfly and butterfly! There are over 5,000 different kinds of true fly in Britain and they are between them quite a tricky bunch of beasts to separate. So what follows are a few of the more interesting ones you will probably come across on your entomological forays.

Body design

The latest thing in insect flying technology, flies take on so many of life's challenges it is quite hard to show one that represents all ... but, here goes, a Blowfly.

Wings – All flies have only one pair of wings

Legs

Eyes – Many flies work with visual cues. They look for food in flowers and search for their mates or prey on the wing.

Mouthparts – These are probably the most variable features of any fly. Flies can do everything from crush pollen, suck nectar, pierce skin to suck blood, stab insects and mop up liquid. Each job requires a different kit of mouthparts.

True flies have the scientific name of *Diptera*, which means two wings, a good example would be the craneflies. They do have a second pair but you have to look very carefully. Towards the abdomen on the thorax is a tiny pair of hair-like projections. They are easy to see in Craneflies because they are quite big, with knobs on, and despite being so small are just as important for flying as the big pair of wings. These reduced and

Below: *Halteres. Look closely at any true fly, here a Cranefly, and you will see these little knob-like organs in place of a proper set of wings. These are halteres and act as highly specialised balancing organs or gyroscopes.*

specialised wings are called halteres and they act as balancing organs, helping the insect remain stable in flight and perform those crackpot aeronautics that flies are so famous for. Flies, in particular those Blowflies that we love to hate so much, are actually the most advanced insects and the very latest thing in body design.

Nearly all flies feed on liquid lunches, whether that is nectar, sweat, urine, the juices from putrefying flesh, or blood, and they have a range of hardware to match these dietary demands.

Next time a Blowfly lands on you take a good look at its mouthparts. They are like a sponge and they will mop

Breeding Blowflies

If a pair of Blowflies were allowed to breed to their full potential and with no predation and their offspring and succeeding generations could do this for four months, the resulting flies would be so many in number you could cover the surface of the Earth up to a depth of 15 metres!

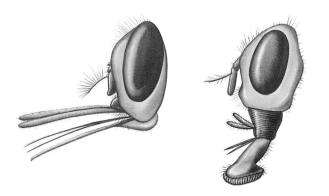

Above: *You can discover any assortment of weird mouth-parts that you could imagine. Between them, flies eat any-thing. Here are the sharp piercing, sucking mouthparts of a biting fly and the sponge-like mouthparts of a Blowfly.*

up anything they fancy; if it's a bit dry they will even spit on their food to help dissolve it and make it more edi-ble. Hoverflies have a range of mouths to reach into dif-ferent depth flowers, while mosquitoes and horseflies have sharp piercing mouthparts and you know exactly what they do with those – bite!

All flies have a complete lifecycle. Baby flies look noth-ing like their parents. We all know these larvae by their popular name of maggots and just like the caterpillar stage of butterflies and moths they are the growing stage, designed to put away as much food as possible.

Mosquitoes – life begins in a pond
A more serene lifecycle is that of the mosquito. In the summer look on the surface of stagnant water, such as water butts and cattle troughs. What you are looking for is a tiny, grey curved raft about 5 mm across. This but-ton of life is a clump of mosquito eggs and if you collect them and some of the same water, you can watch their lifecycle unfold in just a jam jar.

The eggs themselves are fascinating. They are laid in little floating boat shapes of several hundred per clump and they can only float this way up because they have a coating that repels water on all but one end. After only a few days these hatch into tiny, big-headed larvae.

These hang down from the surface by a snorkel on their back ends. They feed on microscopic debris by using the feathery mouthparts to waft food into their mouths by creating a current. In three weeks or so, after moulting their skins several times, they will eventually change into J-shaped pupae. Do not be too perturbed by the fact they can still wriggle around and are highly active, those two funnels stuck on either side of their heads are a couple of snorkels that allow the pupae to breathe while floating under the water's surface.

Watching the lifecycle

You can rear blowflies just like you can butterflies, but it can be quite smelly, so if you want to see the most interesting parts of the lifecycle without the whiff, here is how to go about it.

If you go down to the fishing shop and ask for a quarter of maggots, you will get just that – a tub full of the wriggling larvae of Blowflies. Put them in a clear pot and you keep them warm. One by one they turn into little brown pellets. These are the pupae and a few days later they will burst open and a strange, grotesque thing comes stumbling out. This is an adult fly, without its composure! In a freshly emerged blowfly the head is swollen and pale. The fly inflated its head so it could force its way out of the pupa. Once out, it waits for its skin to harden, wings to unfurl and swollen head to shrink.

You can release the flies when you have finished with them, as keeping them alive and getting them to lay eggs requires smelly, rotten food.

To witness the other part of the lifecycle is easy. Hang up a piece of bacon, the leftovers from the Sunday lunch or even the unfortunate small mam-mal that the cat brought in. As it gets warmer and begins to stink, flies will rush in their hordes. Soon you will notice yellow or white eggs on the meat. These will hatch very soon. Slow hatchers pay the price of not completing their lifecycle or producing stunted adults. Some of the flesh flies will even lay fully formed caterpillars, ready to outcompete and even eat the eggs and larvae of other species!

Below: *Look in any water butt and you will see a mass of little wigglers. These are the filter feeding larvae, the mag-gots of Mosquitoes, which are small but well worth rearing.*

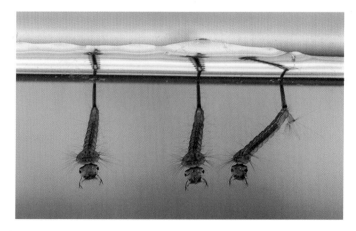

Above: *Catching flies in a sweep net.*

Above: *St Mark's fly. This fly is hard to miss; it dances in huge swarms around trees and hedges. It is named for its habit of turning up around St Mark's day. Look for mated pairs on the ground. Males have the big eyes.*

This stage can last as little as three or four days depending on the water temperature. The adult emerges very quickly as it has to avoid predators.

What use are flies?

Flies are another insect group that people find it hard to enthuse about, but they do a lot more than simply buzz around and spread diseases. The Blowflies and flesh flies are quickly on the scene of a death, laying eggs, and are a formidable power in nature's recycling scheme. They can eat even a large badger carcass in just a week or so.

Hoverflies are the stars of the garden. Appearing to hang in the sunlight by threads, their aerobatics are impressive enough, but consider the pollination services they provide. Their grubs can be found actively scooting about on aphid-infested plants hoovering up 250 or so aphids during their larval career.

There are many other predators and parasites among flies, all battling away to recycle and remove some real pests from the garden. But flies are also fodder for things we do like: Spotted flycatchers, Swallows, Nightjars, bats.

Robber flies
These are the mean-looking muggers of the world of flies, easily recognised by their sheepish ways and appearance. They have a long thin spindly body, long lanky legs often held below and in front of their body and equipped with bristles to snare their prey of other insect life with. They shoot off and catch their prey in mid-flight before returning to the same perch to suck out the contents of their victim.

Cranefly
Walk through long grass or leave a light on in late summer and these gangly insects that seem to be nearly all legs and no body are sure to be seen. The larvae are called leatherjackets and you can often find them if you pull up hunks of moss.

Left: *The fly we all like – the pollen and nectar eating, colourful little chaps we call Hoverflies.*

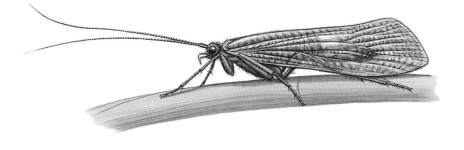

Above: *Caddisfly. They have a complete lifecycle, with larvae and the pupae being entirely aquatic. The larvae, in their camouflaged jackets of sticks, stone and plant fragments, are better known than the adults.*

Horsefly
The owner of the most outlandish eyes in the animal kingdom is sadly, rarely appreciated for its beauty. Horseflies feed on the blood of large mammals.

Winter gnats
A few insects can be seen on the wing even in the middle of winter. These dancing clouds of minute midges are actually a displaying group of males. As soon as a female comes along, they have a little kiss chase before retiring to consummate their relationship.

Caddisflies, Mayflies and Stoneflies
These are a few more of the superficially fly-like flying things, that are not flies. They are very different insects and not even slightly related to each other. The only reason they are together here is because they all have nymphs that live below the surface of the water and if you are having a bit of a dabble about you are likely to find any of them in your pond net.

Caddisfly
These insects are very moth-like in their ways and appearance. Covered in a short, hairy down, this is how they get their family name the *Tricoptera*, which means 'hairy winged'.

Mayfly
Mayflies do not just fly in May and they are not flies! Despite all this confusion there should be no mistaking these winged doilies with any of the other insects you may find hanging around water. Mayflies have three long thread-like tails at the tip of their abdomen and in some species these tails are so long that the adults

Above: *Mayfly. The wings are gorgeous gossamer affairs and are held 'butterfly like' above the body. They glint and glimmer in sunlight and it is romantic on a summer evening to watch these species take part in their nuptial flights.*

dancing over the water look as if they are being worked by submerged puppeteers with wires.

Stonefly
Stoneflies can be confused withCaddisflies as adults but one look at their wings which fold flat on the insects' back and you should be able to tell the difference. The scientific name also rather usefully reflects this; *Plecoptera* means folded wings.

Mayfly for a day
On emerging from the water, the Mayfly nymph ruptures to produce an insect that has wings and can use them right away, handy when the Trout are circling like sharks! This stage is known as a dun but it doesn't last for longer than a maximum of a few hours before the skin splits again and an even more splendid insect also with wings emerges from the old. It is the only insect to have a moult in its winged form. Now it is ready to fly properly and mate. It has no mouthparts and few reserves so the marriage is brief and few live longer than a day. It is this short life span that gives them the scientific name *Ephemeroptera* from the Greek to live a day.

Above: *It is female Mosquitoes only you should be alarmed by – they need a blood meal to fund their developing eggs with proteins.*

Experiment: Catching water babies

Whereas finding the adults is open to a bit of chance (you have to get the season and the weather right), looking for the youth of this bunch is quite exciting and more predictable. The great thing about water is that you can find insects in it all year around, even in the depths of winter.

Stand in the shallows in wellies, upstream from your net. Kick the bottom substrate a few times and you should get a result. Insects in streams tend to hold on tight because current in a stream slows towards the bottom and there is a thin boundary layer between 0.5–0.1 mm above the bottom that is almost stationary. Most of their life is spent hanging on, literally, to the bottom. Among the assortment of oddities now writhing in your

net will be some gadgets a certain Mr. Bond would be proud of. Some of these nymphs will have been dislodged from their hiding places in and among the pebbles and stones. Many are so small that they spend their lives in the shelter of objects on the stream bed. Animals that fall into this category include the tiddly little two-tailed larvae of Stoneflies and the Mayflies (three tails and a rounded body) belonging to the *Beatis* family. Other mayflies are masters of the fast stuff and can be found in the most rapid riffle, because they have a body shaped and designed to hug the contours of a pebble, not even raising an antenna to risk being whipped from their holdings.

To contrast, dip a net through the silty regions of a stream and you will find members of the same groups of insects but more tubular in cross section. Like worms, they are designed to burrow in the sediment. Some, like the family of large mayflies that include *Ephemera danica*, have gills on their back so they can breathe and stay buried at the same time.

I find the best way to find Caddisflies is to turn the contents of your net out into a dish. Once the water has settled out, just stare at it. If a Caddisfly larva is present, it will usually blow its cover by moving. Most slowly amble from place to place, towing with them an ornate case of stones, snail shells, twigs, reeds or sand, depending on the species and the habitat.

The tail of the Scorpion fly

This is a striking fly-like creature that isn't a fly. It has four large wings each marked with distinct dark blotches. Look out for it lurking around hedgerows and gar-

Below and right: *The Scorpion fly is another fly that isn't a fly. Scorpion flies are named after the male's reproductive organs on the end of the abdomen; females have a thinner profile.*

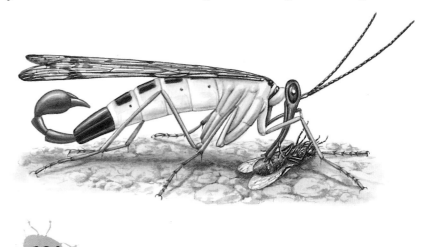

Below: *A close-up of a Lacewing's chiffon-like green wings.*

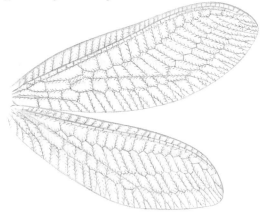

Below: *Keep an eye out when you are out beating bushes and you may find a Lacewing larva munching into an aphid.*

dens, resting on leaves. Its body is long, bright yellow with black bands and it has a head with red eyes and a long pointy beak, with its jaws on the tip.

To add to its rather scary looks, the male has huge pincer-like claspers on the tip of its abdomen, which are often held up and arched slightly over the insect's back. Decomposing animal and plant matter and the occasional chrysalis make up its diet.

Lacewings

In late summer you will almost certainly see one of these green night fairies in a window of your house. They are special insects with large flouncy green chiffon wings, which they hold tent-like over their backs when

at rest. Their eyeballs look like Christmas tree baubles, hence one of their other common names – golden eyes.

Despite their gentle lazy persona, these are top predators and yet another insect that gardeners should welcome. The adults and their larvae are avid fans of aphids. Each lacewing probably consumes a thousand or so in its lifetime.

The larvae can be found among the foliage, where they take on a disguise of aphid husks. Having drained their bodies dry with an evil pair of hollow jaws, they attach the empties to their back – a kind of wolf in sheep's clothing. After running amock this beast will eventually pupate in a silken sock hidden in a crack or crevice to emerge as an adult insect and to start the aphid onslaught once more.

Below: *Lacewings have chiffon-like green wings. You have to look for them in places where their camouflage is less effective than here!*

Below: *The eggs of Lacewings are quite bizarre. They look like a set of pins balancing on their points. It is assumed the idea of the stand is to perturb predators in some way.*

The Little 'uns

This book has really been about the big game of the insect world and not a lot of attention has been given to the really small invertebrates. But they are out there in huge numbers.

Body design

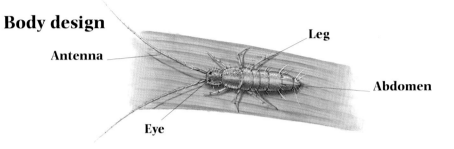

Antenna

Eye

Leg

Abdomen

Funnel fun

Just go out in the garden and take a handful of soil or leaf litter from under the hedge. You will be holding in your palm the whole world for lots of tiny little creatures. To meet them easily, make yourself a tulgren funnel and be sure to have your pooter, lots of specimen pots, field guides and polish up a good high–powered magnifying lens.

You will need:
- *A plastic funnel*
- *A collection vessel (a jam jar or any slippery sided pot will do)*
- *White tissue paper*
- *leaf litter*
- *A bench- or table-light*
See panel below.

What is happening and how this works can be easily explained if you put yourself in the position of anything that might be small and live in the leaf litter.

If you live down there you like it dark. Darkness to a springtail means it is safe from predators. Because springtails are so small, they can lose water very quickly and dry out, so darkness also means dankness. In nature if we have a dry spell and it gets hot the soil dries out – bad news for these tiny creatures of the leaf litter, so they move to a depth where conditions are better.

Your tulgren funnel is recreating these two conditions that they cannot tolerate, heat and light, so the animals move down into the funnel and drop into the collecting jar. This saves you hours and hours of sieving through leaves to find these creatures.

Old birds' nests can also yield a selection of cool pin head creatures.

Making your tulgren funnel

1 Scrunch up the tissue paper and put it in the bottom of the jar. Pop your funnel in the top of the jar.
2 Place the leaf litter in the funnel and then position the lamp close to the leaf litter from above (but not so close you risk burning the house down!).
3 Now wait for a few hours.

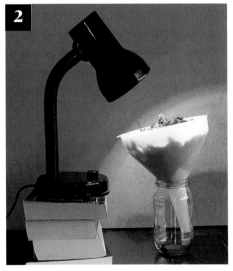

A bristle in the tail

Under the kitchen sink, between the peeling wall paper and an old sponge is not the place you would expect to find a living fossil, but here in damp, cool corners of our homes Silverfish survive.

Silverfish are rarely a pest and tend to go unnoticed unless one gets trapped in a bath or sink during its nocturnal wanderings.

Its silver body is clothed in a layer of pale scales that brush off easily – hence the common name. The multiple tails identify it as a member of the Thysanura – the bristletails.

Scorpion on a pin head

Pseudoscorpions are great looking beasts (see page 65). I will bet that you have them in your own garden, school playground or park hedge. My best catch yet was 19 from a little pile the gardeners missed in the middle of the BBC car park! They are not real scorpions; they have no sting in the tail, they are only 2–5 mm long and they are completely harmless unless you are about 1 mm long! Prey includes small creatures like mites, nematodes and springtails. The Pseudoscorpion overpowers them with a lethal injection given through the tips of its hollow pincers. There are in the region of 25 species in this country.

Spring into action

If Pseudoscorpions are the lions of the leaf litter then the herds of wildebeest and zebra are the springtails. They get just about everywhere and occur in huge numbers. Scientists have found normal soil to contain in the region of 100 million per square metre!

Above: *Silverfish scamper among the cleaning stuff, dusters and old sponges under the sink. They used to do the same when dinosaurs ruled the Earth, although they didn't have kitchen sinks then!*

Springtails are very variable in colour and shape. Some are rounded, others are long and thin, some are dark and velvety looking and others are bright vivid greens and yellows. But despite all this potential confusion, if it is small (2–5 mm), has six legs, no tail and jumps when you touch it, you've definitely got yourself a springtail.

Pop a couple of them into a specimen jar and get a look at their undersides. You will see the mechanism that allows them to pop off so fast when disturbed. Attached at the tip of the abdomen and held folded against its belly is the spring or furcula, a limb that looks a bit like a two-pronged fork. This is clipped in place until needed. Then it is released, pinging down and backwards. The springtail is catapulted forward and away, leaving any slow predator kissing air!

Mighty mites

These are minuscule cousins of spiders and like springtails they get everywhere. They do a lot for the garden, eating fungus threads, grazing on moulds and breaking down dead plant material.

Above, below left and below right: *Just a few of the amazing shapes that springtails take on.*

Spring or furcula

Primeval insect

Look at a Silverfish and you will be staring between the antennae of an insect that would have skittered around the feet of dinosaurs in a virtually unchanged form. These primitive insects could be the ancestors of all insects. From the primeval forest to the peeling wallpaper, Silverfish have survived because they eat pretty much anything organic from plant and animal remains to fungus, mould and even old glue and wallpaper paste.

Further Reading

Bellman, Heiko
A Field Guide to Grasshoppers and Crickets of Britain and Northern Europe
HarperCollins, 1985
ISBN 0 00219 852 5

Brooks, Margaret
A Complete Guide to British Moths
Jonathan Cape, 1991
ISBN 0 22402 195 8

Carter, D., Hargreaves, B.
A Field Guide to Caterpillars of Butterflies and Moths in Britain and Europe
Harpercollins, 1986
ISBN 0 00219 080 X

Chinery, Michael
Butterflies of Britain and Europe
Harpercollins and The Wildlife Trusts, 1998
ISBN 0 00220 059 7

Chinery, Michael
A Field Guide to the Insects of Britain and Northern Europe
Harpercollins, 1993
ISBN 0 00219 918 1

Chinery, Michael
Garden Creepy Crawlies
Whittet Books, 1986
ISBN 0905483 44 8

Chinery, Michael
Insects of Britain and North-West Europe
Harpercollins Pocket Guide, 1993
ISBN 0 00219 137 7

Chinery, Micheal
Spiders
Whittet Books, 1993
ISBN 1 87358 009 6

Easterbrook, Michael
Butterflies of the British Isles – The Lycaenidae
Shire Publications, 2000
ISBN 0 85263 945 7

Easterbrook, Michael
Butterflies of the British Isles – The Nymphalidae
Shire Publications, 2000
ISBN 0 85263 80 9

Easterbrook, Michael
Butterflies of the British Isles – The Pieridae
Shire Publications, 2000
ISBN 0 74780 032 4

Easterbrook, Michael
Hawk-moths of the British Isles
Shire Publications, 2000
ISBN 0 85263 743 8

Ekkehard, Friedrich
Breeding Butterflies and Moths
Harley Books, 1983
ISBN 0 94658 911 9

Gibbons, B.
Dragonflies and Damselflies of Britain and Northern Europe
Country Life Books, 1986
ISBN 0 600 35841 0

Gibbons, B.
Field Guide to the Insects of Britain and Northern Europe
The Crowood Press, 1996
ISBN 1 85223 895 X

Hammond, Nicholas (Series Editor)
The Wildlife Trusts Guide to Butterflies and Moths
New Holland Publishers, 2002
ISBN 1 85974 959 3

Hammond, Nicholas (Series Editor)
The Wildlife Trusts Guide to Garden Wildlife
New Holland Publishers, 2002
ISBN 1 85974 961 5

Hammond, Nicholas (Series Editor)
The Wildlife Trusts Guide to Insects
New Holland Publishers, 2002
ISBN 1 85974 962 3

Hammond, Nicholas (Series Editor)
The Wildlife Trusts Handbook of Garden Wildlife
New Holland Publishers, 2002
ISBN 1 85974 960 7

Jones, D.
The Country Life Guide to Spiders of Britain and Northern Europe
Country Life Books, 1983
ISBN 0 60035 665 5

Kerney. M. P., Cameron, R. A. D.
A Field Guide to the Land Snails of Britain and North-West Europe
Harpercollins, 1979
ISBN 0 00219 676 X

Murphy, Frances
Keeping Spiders, Insects and Other Land Invertebrates in Captivity
Bartholomew, 1980
ISBN 0 70288 020 5

Nancarrow, Loren, Hogan Taylor, Janet
The Worm Book
Ten Speed Press, 1998
ISBN 0 89815 994 6

North, Ray
Ants
Whittet Books, 1996
ISBN 1 87358 025 8

Oxford, R.
Minibeast Magic – Kind-hearted Capture Techniques for Invertebrates
A Yorkshire Wildlife Trust Publication, 1999
ISBN 9 780950 946020

Packham, Chris
Chris Packham's Back Garden Nature Reserve
New Holland Publishers, 2001
ISBN 1 85974 520 2

Porter, Jim
The Colour Identification Guide to Caterpillars of the British Isles
Viking, 1997
ISBN 0 67087 509 0

Robert, Michael J.
The Collins Field Guide to the Spiders of Britain and Northern Europe
HarperCollins, 1995
ISBN 0 00219 981 5

Skinner, B.
Colour Identification Guide to Moths of the British Isles
Viking, 1984
ISBN 0 67080 354 5

Skinner, G.
Ants of the British Isles
Shire Publications, 2000
ISBN 0 85263 896 5

Thomas, Jeremy; Lewington, Richard
The Butterflies of Britain and Ireland
Dorling Kindersley, 1991
ISBN 0 86318 591 6

Tyler, John
Glow-worms
Tyler-Scagell, 1994
ISBN 0 95235 260 5

Wardhaugh, A. A.
Land Snails of the British Isles
Shire Publications, 2000
ISBN 0 74780 027 8

Dig a Pond for Dragonflies
British Dragonfly Society
(available from Mrs J. Silsby
1 Haydn Avenue
Purley
Surrey GR8 4AG)

Series of *Naturalists' Handbooks*
Richmond Publishing Co. Ltd.

Useful Addresses

The Amateur Entomologists' Society
PO Box 8774
London SW7 5ZG
Email: aes@theaes.org
Website: www.theaes.org

Bees, Wasps and Ants Recording Society
Membership Secretary: David Baldock
Nightingales
Haslemere Road
Milford
Surrey GU8 5BN
Website: website.lineone.net/
~ammophila/

British Arachnological Society
Secretary: Dr Helen J. Read
2 Egypt Wood Cottages
Egypt Lane
Farnham Common
Bucks SL2 3LE
Tel: 01753 645791
Fax: 01753 646699
Email: secretary@britishspiders.org.uk
Website: http://www.salticus.demon
.co.uk

British Butterfly Conservation Society
Manor Yard
East Lulworth
near Wareham
Dorset BH20 5QP
Tel: 01929 400209
Fax: 01929 400210
Email: info@butterfly-conservation.org
Website: www.butterfly-conservation.
org

Virginia Cheeseman
3 Sutton Road
Hounslow
Middlesex TW5 0PG
Tel/Fax: 020 8572 0414
Website: members.aol.com/
vcheeseman

British Dragonfly Society
Secretary: Dr W. H. Wain
The Haywain
Hollywater Road
Bordon
Hants GU35 0AD
Email:
bdswebmaster@hanslope.demon.co.uk
Website: www.dragonflysoc.org.uk

Brunel Microscopes (BR) Limited
Unit 12 Enterprise Estate
Chippenham, Wilts SN14 6QA
Tel. 01249 462 655
Fax 01249 445 156
Email: brunelmicro@compuserve.com
Website: www.brunelmicroscopes.
co.uk

Conchological Society of Great Britain and Ireland
Mike Weideli
35 Bartlemy Road
Newbury
Berks RG14 6LD
Tel: 01635 42190
Fax: 01635 820904
Email: membership@conchsoc.org
Website: www.conchsoc.org

Gordon's Entomological Home Page
Website: www.earthlife.net/insects/

Marris House Nets
54 Richmond Park Avenue,
Queen's Park
Bournemouth BH8 9DR
Tel: 01202 515238
Fax: 01202 510303
Website: www.pwbelg.clara.net/marris

The Microscope Shop
Oxford Road
Sutton Scotney
Winchester
Hants SO21 3JG

Oxford Bee Company Ltd
40 Arthur Street
Loughborough
Leics LE11 3AY
Tel: 01509 261654
Fax: 01509 261672
Email: info@oxbeeco.com
Website: fp.oxbeeco.f9.co.uk

Small Life Supplies
Station Buildings
Station Road
Bottesford
Notts NG13 0EB
Tel: 01949 842446
Fax: 01949 843036
Website: www.small-life.co.uk

Watkins and Doncaster the Naturalists
PO Box 5
Cranbrook
Kent TN18 5EZ
(General naturalist supplies – nets,
boxes, moth traps, pooters, etc.)
Tel: 01580 753133
Fax: 01580 754054
Email: robin.ford@virgin.net
Website: www.watdon.com

The Wildlife Trusts
The Kiln
Waterside
Mather Road
Newark
Notts NG24 1WT
Tel: 0870 0367711
Fax: 0870 0360101
Email: info@wildlife-trusts.cix.co.uk
Website: www.wildlifetrusts.org

Wildlife Watch
(Contact details for Wildlife Watch are
the same as for The Wildlife Trusts)
Email: watch@wildlife-trusts.cix.co.uk
Website: www.wildlifewatch.org.uk

Glossary

abdomen: The part of the body of an arthropod behind the thorax.

aerial plankton: Floating or drifting organisms, especially very small ones, found in the atmosphere.

annelids: A group of worms with bodies divided into segments, such as earthworms, ragworms and leeches.

antenna: One of a pair of sensory organs (feelers) on the heads of insects etc., used for smell taste and touch.

arachnid: An arthropod belonging to the class Arachnida, with eight legs and simple eyes.

arachnophobia: Irrational fear of spiders.

arthropods: Invertebrates with segmented bodies and jointed legs, including the insects, crustaceans and arachnids; the largest group in the animal kingdom.

carapace: The upper shell of a crustacean, which is hard.

cephalothorax: The fused thorax and head possessed by arthropods and crustaceans.

chitin: An insoluble chemical, which is the main constituent of the exoskeleton of arthropods.

chrysalis: A pupa of a butterfly or moth

claustral cell: A small area resembling a cloister or enclosed space.

clitellum: A raised band around the body of some worms, containing reproductive segments.

crustaceans: A group of arthropods, mainly marine, including woodlice and shrimps.

cuticle: The protective outer layer of an insect.

elytron: The outer hard wing-case of some insects.

entomology: The branch of zoology that deals with the study of insects.

epiphragm: The layer of hard secretion, which closes a snail's shell before it hibernates.

exoskeleton: An arthropod's external body covering giving protection and support of internal organs.

exuvia: Cast skins, or shed outer parts of insects.

formic acid: A volatile acid produced by various ants.

formicarium: An artificial ant house.

furcula: The forked end of the abdomen of a springtail, which it uses to jump.

gall: An abnormal growth of plant tissue, usually caused by insects.

gastropod: Molluscs of the class Gastropoda, including slugs and snails, typically having a flattened muscular foot.

geometrids: Moths of the family Geometridae. The caterpillars move by stretching then hunching their bodies.

gill: Respiratory organ of aquatic invertebrates, functioning similar to fish gills.

gland: A small animal organ secreting substances, often aromatic.

hermaphrodite: An animal having both female and male sexual organs, like snails and worms.

hibernation: Spending the winter in a state of dormancy or deep sleep.

humus: The organic part of soil, formed by the breaking down of plant materials.

hymenoptera: Members of a large order of insects, including the bees, wasps, and ants.

ichneumon: Members of a family of hymenoptera insects that lay their eggs inside other insects.

imago: The final form of an insect after it has developed through the various stages of its metamorphosis.

invertebrate: An animal lacking a spinal column or backbone; spiders, snails, etc.

isopods: A group of crustaceans that includes the woodlice.

larva: A development stage of an insect lasting from the time of leaving the egg until its transformation into a pupa, displaying little similarity to the adult.

lepidoptera: Butterflies and moths; members of a large order of insects having four scale-covered wings.

metamorphosis: The transformation in several developmental stages that some animals undergo to become an adult, in which there is a complete alteration of form and habit.

mucus: A non-water soluble slimy substance, secreted by glands and membranes of animals for lubrication, protection, etc.

nymph: An insect larva that resembles an adult but immature.

ocellus: Each of the small simple, as distinct from compound, eyes of insects.

ovipositor: A specialised egg-laying organ at the end of the abdomen of the female of some insects, often adapted for stinging, piercing, or sawing.

palp: A long appendage near invertebrates' mouths used for movement, taste or touch.

parasite: An animal living in or on another animal or plant, and feeding directly from it, harming its host.

pheromone: A chemical released by an animal, which causes a response when detected by another animal of the same species.

pollination: The transport or depositing of pollen on a flower by an insect, which leads to fertilisation of the plant.

predator: An animal that catches and eats other animals.

proboscis: A long, tube-like, flexible mouth part of many insects.

pupa: An insect in the developmental stage, between the larva and the adult, sometimes known as chrysalis.

radula: A movable toothed structure in the mouth of a mollusc, used for scraping off and drawing in food.

rostrum: The elongated mouthparts of some insects.

scopula: A small, dense tuft of hairs.

seta: A stiff hair or bristle, or an appendage resembling a bristle.

spinneret: An organ through which the silk or thread of spiders, silkworms and other insects is produced.

spiracle: A pore leading into the trachea of an insect.

stabilimentum: A thick band of silk that runs across the webs of some spiders.

stridulation: The sound made by male grasshoppers and crickets, produced by rubbing a part of the body against another.

thorax: The middle section of an arthropod's body, between the abdomen and the head.

trachea: A tube which conveys air direct to the tissues leading from a spiracle in an arthropod.

uropod: An abdominal appendage like an antenna, found in some insects and crustaceans.

vestigial: An animal organ that has become functionless in the course of evolution.

vivarium: A structure prepared for keeping animals under their natural conditions, for observation or study.

Index

Page numbers in **bold** refer to illustrations

Allolobophora
  A. longa 25, 27, **27**
  A. nocturna 25
Ammophilia sabulosa 102–3
Amourobius **59**
Androniscus niger 44, **44**
Annelids 19
ant,
  Black garden **111**, 116
  Black pavement 110, **112**, 116
  Red 116, **116**
  Yellow lawn **116**
  Wood 110, 113, **114**, 116
ants 110–17, **110–17**
  body design 111, 112, 116
  lifecycle 110–13, **111**
  nests 110, **111**, 112, **113**
Apanteles 84, 103
aphids 113, 118, **118**, 119, 120, 122, **122**
  as food 125, 126, **126**, **135**
Apis mellifera 105
arachnids 45, 50–65, **50–65**
Araneus
  A. diadematus 62, **62**
  A. quadratus 62
Argiope bruennichi 58, 63, **63**
Argyroneta aquatica 54, 64, **64**
arthropods 11, **38**
  arachnids 45, 50–65, **50–65**
  centipedes/millipedes **10**, **11**, 45, 46–9, **46–9**
  exoskeleton 13, 38, 39, **39**, 40, **40**, 48, 51
  insects 11, 66–137, **66–137**
  woodlice **11**, 39–45, **38–45**
  see also bugs
Assassin bug **123**

Beatis 134
bee,
  Buff-tailed bumble 108, **108**
  Bumble 105, **105**, 107, 108
  Honey **104**, 105, 106, **106**, 107, **107**, 108
  Mason **102**
bees 104–9, **104–9**
  banks/boxes **104**, 108–9, **109**
  body design 104–5, **105**, 107
  lifecycle 104, 107, 108, **108**, **109**

nests 105, 107, 108
stings 104, 105
swarms **108**
beetle,
  Chafer 124
  Devil's coach-horse 128, **128**
  Great diving **128**
  Ground 32
  Lesser stag **11**
  Sailor 129
  Soldier 129, **129**
  Stag 124
  Tiger 125, **125**
beetles **11**, **67**, 124–9, **124–9**
  body design 124, 125
  lifecycle **125**
bird food 20, **20**, 26, 31, **32**, 112, **112**, 132
Blackbird 31, 33
Blackfly 119, **119**, 120
Bombus
  B. hortorum **105**
  B. pascuorum **107**
  B. terrestris 108, **108**
bugs 118–23, **118–23**
  aphids 118, **118**, 119, 120, 122, **122**
  arthropods 11, **11**, 38–65, **38–65**, 66–137, **66–137**
  body design 118, **118**, 123, 136, **136**
  insects 11, 66–137, **66–137**
  legless 11, 18–37, **18–37**
  lifecycle 118–20, **119**
butterflies/moths 68–85, **68–85**
  body design 68–9, **69**, 71, 72–4, **72**, 73, 75, 76–7, **76**, 83
  caterpillars 68, **69**, 70–74, **71–5**, **76**, 82–3, 84, 85, 103
butterfly,
  Cabbage white 74, 84, **84**
  Comma 73, **74**
  Dingy skipper 68
  Gatekeeper 72, 77
  Hedge brown **56**
  Holly blue **81**
  Large white 84, **84**, 103
  Meadow brown 72, 77
  Orange tip 80–81, **81**
  Painted lady **69**
  Peacock 73, 75, 76, 84–5, **84**

Small copper **76**
Small tortoiseshell 73, 74, 75, **75**, 84–5, **84**
Small white 84, **84**
Red admiral **84**, 85
butterfly nets 69, **70**, 91

Cantharis
  C. fusca 129
  C. livida 129
  C. rustica 129
captive specimens
  beetles 125, 127–8, **127**
  bugs 136, **136**
  butterflies/moths 69, 80–83, **80–83**
  caterpillar boxes 82, **82**
  crickets/grasshoppers 93, 95–7
  dragonflies/damselflies 91, **91**
  environmental needs 13
  flies 131, 134
  formicariums 110, 114–16, **114–16**
  ladybirds 126
  restraining of 14, **14–15**
  snails 30
  spiders 60, **60**
  tegenariums 60, **60**
  wasps 102
  wormerys 19, 22, **22–3**
caterpillars see butterflies/moths
centipede,
  Common **47**
  Garden 49, **49**
centipedes **10**, **11**, 46–7, **46–7**, 48–9, **48–9**
  body design 46–7, 48, **48**
Cerceris 103
chaser, Broad-bodied **10**, **87**
Chrysis 103
Coleoptera **67**
communication techniques 106, **106**, 117
cricket,
  Bush 95, **95**, 96, 97
  Dark bush 93, **96**
  Green bush 96
  Oak bush 94, **97**
  Speckled bush 93, **97**
cricket tongs 93, 97
crickets/grasshoppers 92–7, **92–7**
  body design 92–3, **93**, 94–7, **94–5**
  lifecycle 94–6, **95**

Crustaceans 39
cuckoo spit 120, **120**
cyclops **38**, 45, **45**
Cyclosa conica **58**

damselfly,
  Common azure **10**, **87**
  Large red **87**
damselflies see dragonflies/damselflies
Dendrobaena subrubicunda 27
Diptera 130
dragonflies/damselflies 86–91, **86–91**
  body design 86–8, **87–8**, 90, **90**
  lifecycle 86, 88–90, **88–90**, 91
dragonfly,
  Golden-ringed **87**
  Hawker **86**, 89
Dysdera 45

earthworms see worms
earwigs 66
Ephemeroptera 133
equipment **8**, 12–17, **12–17**, 82, **82**, 83, 91, **91**
  beating trays 71, **71**, 119
  bee boxes **104**
  collection jars 15, 17, 69
  cricket tongs 93
  magnifying lenses 13, **13**
  moth traps 80, **80**
  nets 15
    butterfly 69, **70**, 91
    pond 91, **91**
    sweep 97, **132**
  pitfall traps 13, 127–8, **127**
  pooters 16–17, **16–17**
  torches 21, 24
  tulgren funnels 136, **136**
  tweezers/forceps 15
exoskeletons 13, 38, 39, **39**, 40, **40**, 48, 51
experiments
  with ants 117, **117**
  with bees 108, 109
  with bugs 120
  with butterflies/moths 65, 77–80, **78**
  with dragonflies/damselflies 88
  with flies 134
  with slugs/snails 33–7, **34**
  with spiders 55, **55**, 61, **61**

with woodlice 42
exuviae 90, **90**

flies 130–35, **130–35**
　body design 130–31,
　　130–31, 135, **135**
　life cycle 130–2, **131**, 133,
　　134, 135, **135**
fly,
　Blowfly 130, **130**, 131, **131**,
　　132
　Caddisfly 133, **133**, 134
　Cranefly 130, **130**, 132
　Horsefly 133
　Hoverfly **9**, 132, **132**
　Lacewing 135, **135**
　Mayfly 133, **133**, 134
　Mosquito 131, **131**, **134**
　Robber 132
　St Mark's **132**
　Scorpion 134–5, **134**
　Stonefly 133, 134
　Winter gnat 133
Formicine 116
Freshwater shrimp 45, **45**

gall,
　Artichoke 102, **102**
　Common spangle 102, **102**
　Marble 102, **103**
　Oak apple 102
　Silk button **102**
Gastropods 28
Geophilomorphs 49
grasshopper,
　Common field **95**
　Marsh 94
　Meadow **97**
grasshoppers see
　crickets/grasshoppers
Greenfly 120

Haplophilus subterraneus **47**,
　49, **49**
harvestmen 65, **65**
hedgehogs 31, **32**, 45
Hemiptera 118
Heterocera 68
Hymenoptera **67**, 98, 104

Icheneumon 103
insects 11, 66–137, **66–137**
　ants 110–17, **110–17**
　bees 104–9, **104–9**
　beetles **67**, 124–9, **124–9**
　body design 66–7, **66–7**
　butterflies/moths **56**, 68–85,
　　68–85
　crickets/grasshoppers 92–7,
　　92–7
　dragonflies/damselflies
　　86–91, **86–91**

flies 130–35, **130–35**
　wasps **11**, **51**, **67**, 98–103,
　　98–103
　see also bugs
invertebrates 10, 38
Isopods 39

ladybirds **110**, 124, 125–6,
　126
Lasius niger 110
legless species 11
　slugs/snails **11**, 28–37,
　　28–37
　worms 18–27, **18–27**
Leiobunum rotundum 65, **65**
Lepidoptera 68
Linyphilids 60
Lumbricus terrestris 21

Maybug 128–9
millipede,
　Flat-backed 49, **49**
　Pill 49, **49**
　Snake **47**, 49, **49**
millipedes **11**, 47–9, **47–9**
Misumena vatia 64, **64**
mites 65, **65**, 137
molluscs 28
moth,
　Cinnabar 73
　Elephant hawk 68, **72**
　Emperor 85, **85**
　Eyed hawk **72**, 85, **85**
　Garden tiger **79**
　Herald **69**
　Leopard **83**
　Lime hawk 85, **85**
　Magpie 73, **79**
　Mother-of-pearl 85
　Poplar hawk 85, **85**
　Small emerald **77**
moths see butterflies/moths
Myriapods 46
Myrmicine 116

Necrophloephagus longicornis **10**
Nemastoma bimaculatum **65**
Nymphalid 75

ocelli 40, **40**, 66
Odonata 86
Oligochaetes 20
Opiliones 65
Orthoptera 92

parasitic wasps 84, 103, **103**
Pholcus phalangioides 62, **62**
pitfall traps 13, 127–8, **127**
pooters (suction traps) 16–17,
　16–17
Pardosa amentata 54
Polydesmids 48, 49, **49**

pond skaters **67**, 121–2
Porcellio 45
　P. scaber 44, **44**
psuedoscorpions 65, **65**, 137

red spider mites 65, **65**
Rhagonycha fulva 129
Rhopalocera 68
rove beetles 128

Saltatoria 92
Salticus scenincus 52, 63, **63**
Saucer bug 123
Segestria florentina 55
sheep ticks 65, **65**
shield bugs 121, **121**
shrews 31, 45
Silverfish 137, **137**
slug,
　Great black 33, 37, **37**
　Shelled 37, **37**
slugs/snails **11**, 28–37, **28–37**
　body design 28–33, **29**, **33**,
　　38
　lifecycle 30–31, **30–31**
　slime 28, **29**, 30, 33, 34–5,
　　34
snail,
　Banded **35**
　Brown-lipped **35**, 36, **36**
　Door 36, **36**
　Garlic 31
　Garden 31, **34**, 35, 36, **36**
　Great pond 30, 33, **33**, 37,
　　37
　Hairy 36, **36**
　Ramshorn 37, **37**
　Strawberry 36, **36**
　White-lipped **35**, 36
sound production 67, 94, **94**,
　122
spangle gall,
　Common 102, **102**
　Silk button 102, **102**
spider,
　Crab 53, **56**, 64, **64**
　Daddy long legs 62, **62**
　Garden cross **59**, 62, **62**
　House **50**, 52, **52**, 60, **60**,
　　62–3, **63**
　Labyrinth **53**
　Mesh web 63, **63**
　Nursery web **55**, **59**, 63,
　　63
　Orb web 55, 57, 58, **58**, 61
　Spotted wolf **54**
　Wasp **58**, 63, **63**
　Water 54, 64, **64**
　Wolf 51, 52, 53, 54–5, **54**
　Woodlouse 51, 62, **62**
　Zebra 52, 63, **63**
spiders 50–64, **50–64**

body design 50–4, **50–53**,
　56, **56**, 63, **64**
　lifecycle 52, **52**, 54–5, **54**,
　　59, **59**, 63, 62
　webs/strands **53**, 54, 56–8,
　　56–9, 60, 61, **61**, 62, 63
springtails 137, **137**
Staphylinids 128

thrush,
　Mistle **20**, 31
　Song 31, **32**
toads 31, 45

vole,
　Bank 31
　Field 31

wasp,
　Common **100**
　Opium 103
　Ruby-tail **102**, 103
　Sand 102–3
　Spider-hunting **51**
wasps **11**, **51**, **67**, 84, 98–103,
　98–103
　body design 104
　lifecycle 98, 99–101, **100**,
　　103, **103**
　nests 98–101, **99–101**, 107
　social 98–102, 106, **106**
　solitary 98, 102–3, 104
　stings 98, 103, 104
Water boatman **122**, 123
　Lesser 122, 123
water bugs 121–3, **121–3**
water crickets 121–2
Water flea 45, **45**
Water louse 40, **41**, 45, **45**
water measurers 121–2, **121**
Water scorpion 123, **123**
water snails 30, 31, 33, **33**,
　36, 37
woodlice **11**, 39–45, **38–45**
woodlouse,
　Common 44, **44**
　Pill 40, 44, **44**
worm,
　Angler's red 27, **27**
　Brandling **18**, 27, **27**
　Common earthworm 21, **26**,
　　27
　Glow worm 32, 129, **129**
worms 18–27, **18–27**
　body design 19, **19**, 20–21,
　　20
　burrows/burrowing 18–19,
　　20–21, 24
　casts 25–6, **25**
　lifecycle 19, 21–2, **21**

Zygiella 58, **58**

Acknowledgements

Author's acknowledgements

A big thank you goes out to my parents Sandy and Steve and my brother Paul who have tolerated my multi-legged friends, especially the silk moths in the wardrobe and the Tarantulas under the bed, for the best part of 29 years!

I would also like to thank all those at New Holland especially Jo Hemmings for encouraging me to write this book and to Lorna Sharrock and Mike Unwin for not shouting at me and getting too cross when I give them some pathetic excuse for not meeting a deadline!!

My neighbours Rob, Julia, Madeleine and Joe for allowing me and photographer Dave Cottridge to invade their pond, to photograph Southern hawker dragonflies emerging!!

Nick Baker

Photographic acknowledgements

All photographs by David M. Cottridge, with the exception of the following:
Melissa Edwards: front cover, 6, 8, 12, 28, 46, 68, 71, 92, 99, 104, 114(bl, br), 115, 119(t), 132(t)
Richard Revels: 9, 18, 21, 23(br), 24, 31, 33, 38, 41(bl), 42, 53, 56, 59, 60(br), 67(t,b), 72(b), 74,76, 79, 81, 95, 96, 98, 101, 107, 108, 109(t), 110, 112, 113, 114(t), 119(b), 121, 122, 123, 126, 131, 134, 135, 137
Stephen Dalton: 64
Jason Smalley: 34(b)

(t= top; b=bottom; c=centre; l=left; r=right)

Artwork acknowledgements

All artwork by Wildlife Art Agency, with the exception of the following:
Sheila Hadley: 29, 36(br), 66, 118(t), 125(t), 129
David Daly: 20 (l), 32, 112

(t= top; b=bottom; c=centre; l=left; r=right)